Easy Microsoft® Access 97

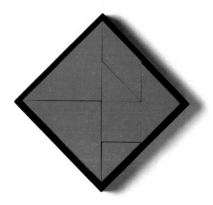

Jeffry Byrne

Easy Microsoft Access 97

Library of Congress Catalog Card Number: 96-71426

International Standard Book Number: 0-7897-1027-7

99 98 97   8 7 6 5 4 3 2 1

Interpretation of the printing code: the rightmost double-digit number is the year of the book's first printing; the rightmost single-digit number is the number of the book's printing. For example, a printing code of 97-1 shows that this copy of the book was printed during the first printing of the book in 1997.

Screen reproductions in this book were created by means of the program Collage Complete from Inner Media, Inc, Hollis, NH.

Printed in the United States of America

Dedication

To my wife, Marisa. Without her help and years of support this would not have been completed.

Credits

Publisher
Roland Elgey

Publishing Manager
Lynn E. Zingraf

Editorial Services Director
Elizabeth Keaffaber

Managing Editor
Michael Cunningham

Director of Marketing
Lynn E. Zingraf

Acquisitions Editor
Martha O'Sullivan

Technical Specialist
Nadeem Muhammed

Product Development Specialist
Melanie Palaisa

Technical Editor
Don Funk

Production Editor
Tom Lamoureux

Book Designers
Barbara Kordesh
Ruth Harvey

Cover Designers
Dan Armstrong
Kim Scott

Production Team
Stephen Adams
Tammy Ahrens
Kathleen Caulfield
Kevin Cliburn
Tammy Graham
Jason Hand
Pete Lippincott
Tom Missler
Erich Richter
Laura Robbins
Holly Wittenberg

Indexer
Chris Barrick

Composed in *Syntax* and *New Century Schoolbook* by Que Corporation

We'd Like to Hear from You!

As part of our continuing effort to produce books of the highest possible quality, Que would like to hear your comments. To stay competitive, we *really* want you, as a computer book reader and user, to let us know what you like or dislike most about this book or other Que products.

You can mail comments, ideas, or suggestions for improving future editions to the address below, or send us a fax at (317) 581-4663. For the online inclined, Macmillan Computer Publishing has a forum on CompuServe (type **GO QUEBOOKS** at any prompt) through which our staff and authors are available for questions and comments. The address of our Internet site is **http://www.mcp.com/que** (World Wide Web).

In addition to exploring our forum, please feel free to contact me personally to discuss your opinions of this book: I'm **73353,2061** on CompuServe, and I'm **mpalaisa@que.mcp.com** on the Internet.

Although we cannot provide general technical support, we're happy to help you resolve problems you encounter related to our books, disks, or other products. If you need such assistance, please contact our Tech Support department at 800-545-5914 ext. 3833.

To order other Que or Macmillan Computer Publishing books or products, please call our Customer Service department at 800-835-3202 ext. 666.

Thanks in advance—your comments will help us to continue publishing the best books available on computer topics in today's market.

Melanie Palaisa
Product Development Specialist
Que Corporation
201 W. 103rd Street
Indianapolis, Indiana 46290
USA

About the Author

Jeffry Byrne has been working and teaching about computers, and particularly about database applications, for over fifteen years. He is the author of numerous computer software books in several languages, including; Que's *Paradox QuickStart*, *Using CA-Simply Money*, *Easy Access for Windows*, *Easy Access for Windows 95*, *Easy Access 97*. He has also contributed to Que's *Using QuickBooks for Windows*, and *Using PowerPoint 4*. He has also written other books on Microsoft SQL Server, and other popular database and spreadsheet programs. He has worked on the beta test teams for most of these products and for several other accounting and database software organizations. When not writing about and testing software, Jeff works as the product/purchasing manager for a Portland, Oregon-based network VAR and computer retailer. You can contact Jeff through CompuServe (71553,1660).

Acknowledgments

I would like to thank Martha O'Sullivan for allowing me to continue updating this book, and to Melanie Palaisa for her work in editing this work. Also to Tom Lamoureux for his work in keeping things to schedule and to Don Funk for his excellent work in ensuring the accuracy of this book. Also to all of the other people at Que who have had a hand in this work.

Trademarks

Contents

Introduction   **2**

Part I: Learning the Basics   7

1	Installing Access	10
2	Starting Access from the Start Button	14
3	Opening an Existing Database	17
4	Using Menu Commands	19
5	Using Toolbar Buttons and Tabs	22
6	Getting Help	25
7	Using Context-Sensitive Help	30
8	Using the Office Assistant	32
9	Exiting Access	36
10	Creating a Shortcut for Access on Your Desktop	38

Part II: Designing and Creating an Access Database   43

11	Creating a New Database	46
12	Using the Table Wizard	49
13	Adding a New Field in Design View	54
14	Working with Numbers	57
15	Using a Yes/No Field	60
16	Saving the New Table Definition	63
17	Opening a Table	65
18	Changing a Field Name	67
19	Moving a Field Within a Table	70
20	Inserting a Field	73
21	Adding a New Field in Datasheet View	76
22	Deleting a Field	78
23	Building a Table from Scratch	80

Part III: Entering and Editing Data   85

24	Entering New Information in a Table	90
25	Copying Information from Another Record	94
26	Editing Data in a Field	97
27	Undoing an Edit	100
28	Searching for Information	103
29	Replacing Selected Information	108
30	Sorting Records	111
31	Using Filters	113
32	Filtering by Form	115
33	Deleting a Selected Record	118
34	Resizing Rows and Columns	120
35	Freezing and Unfreezing Columns	123
36	Hiding and Unhiding Columns	126

Part IV: Using Database Forms   131

37	Using the New Object AutoForm	134
38	Building a Form with a Wizard	136
39	Opening the Form Design View Window	140
40	Adding Fields to a Form	142
41	Creating Labels and Entering Text	146
42	Using a Combo Box	149
43	Adding a List Box	154
44	Moving Groups of Objects	158
45	Editing a Label	161
46	Using an Option Button	163
47	Adding Pop-Up Tip Text to Fields	167
48	Saving Your New Form	170
49	Opening a Form	172
50	Entering and Editing Information with a Form	174
51	Changing the Field Order	178

Contents

Part V: Getting Information from a Database   183

52	Creating a Select Query	186
53	Using the Crosstab Query	191
54	Selecting Records with Wild Cards	195
55	Selecting Records with an "OR" Criterion	198
56	Selecting Records with More than One Criterion	201
57	Using Arithmetic Operators	204

Part VI: Creating and Using Reports   209

58	Building a Report with a Wizard	212
59	Creating a Report in Design View	217
60	Using Groups and Sorting	221
61	Using Labels in a Report	225
62	Printing a Report	230

Part VII: Combining Information   233

63	Building a Permanent Relationship Between Tables	236
64	Using a Query with Two Tables	239
65	Creating a Report with a Query	242

Index   248

Introduction

This book is designed with you, the beginner, in mind. The tasks in this book are designed to help you get up and running by guiding you through many common database operations.

What You Can Do With Access

Every day you work with many different databases: your personal phone directory, a customer list, a product catalog, employee records, or information in a filing cabinet. With Microsoft Access 97 you can build a database that can store and manipulate any information that you need to use. You can use Microsoft Access 97 for many tasks, including these:

- Creating a personal address and phone list.
- Maintaining mailing lists and labels.
- Keeping a list of customer contacts.
- Building sales reports.
- Creating a sales order database.
- Building an inventory control system.

Easy Microsoft Access 97 is divided into seven parts. Each part is concerned with a different aspect of Microsoft Access 97, and each successive part is built on information that you learn from earlier parts.

While Microsoft Access 97 can be easy to use, it is still a complex database program. Part I, "Learning the Basics," provides an introduction to installing the program and many common features and tasks.

You can store any type of information in a Microsoft Access 97 table. You can easily build a table to store any information that you want to track. You can use tables to store data about employees, inventory, orders, stamps, coins, or your plants in your yard. In Part II, "Designing and Creating an Access Database," you learn to create a table.

You can quickly and easily change information in the database. If a supplier's phone number or address changes, you simply have to change this information in the supplier's table. Microsoft Access 97 changes the new address and phone number on all forms and reports. These tasks are covered in Part III, "Entering and Editing Data."

You can create a form to display information in a familiar way. By using forms to show the information from a table, you can easily view an entire record in a familiar format. If you use a paper form, you can easily design a Microsoft Access 97 form that looks and works like the form you already use. These tasks are covered in Part IV, "Using Database Forms."

You can choose selected records from your database that meet criteria that you specify. For example, instead of searching through all your customer files to find who bought green widgets last month, simply query Microsoft Access 97 to find and display this information. Tasks that show you how to build a query are included in Part V, "Getting Information from a Database."

You can create printed reports from the information contained in your database. For example, you can print a report that displays a summary of your sales over the last month and groups the information by salesperson or items sold. These tasks are covered in Part VI, "Creating and Using Reports."

You can create even more powerful forms and reports by combining information from more than one source. By using a query to select data from more than one table, you can view, add, or edit information in each of the tables. Forms and reports can use a query to select and display related information from combined sources. These tasks are covered in Part VII, "Combining Information."

Task Sections

The Task sections include numbered steps that tell you how to accomplish certain tasks such as saving a workbook or filling a range. The numbered steps walk you through a specific example so that you can learn the task by doing it.

Big Screen

At the beginning of each task is a large screen that shows how the computer screen will look after you complete the procedure that follows in that task. Sometimes the screen shows a feature discussed in that task, however, such as a shortcut menu.

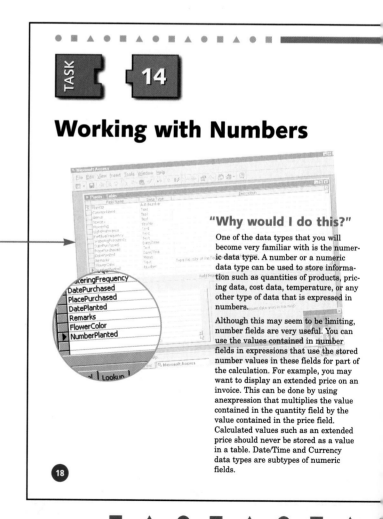

TASK

14

Working with Numbers

"Why would I do this?"

One of the data types that you will become very familiar with is the numeric data type. A number or a numeric data type can be used to store information such as quantities of products, pricing data, cost data, temperature, or any other type of data that is expressed in numbers.

Although this may seem to be limiting, number fields are very useful. You can use the values contained in number fields in expressions that use the stored number values in these fields for part of the calculation. For example, you may want to display an extended price on an invoice. This can be done by using anexpression that multiplies the value contained in the quantity field by the value contained in the price field. Calculated values such as an extended price should never be stored as a value in a table. Date/Time and Currency data types are subtypes of numeric fields.

18

Step-by-Step Screens

Each task includes a screen shot for each step of a procedure that shows how the computer screen will look at each step in the process.

Task 14: Working with Numbers

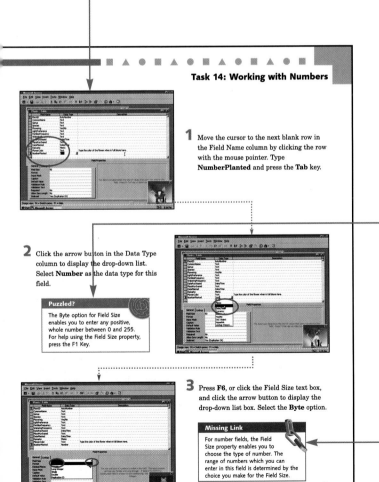

1 Move the cursor to the next blank row in the Field Name column by clicking the row with the mouse pointer. Type **NumberPlanted** and press the **Tab** key.

2 Click the arrow button in the Data Type column to display the drop-down list. Select **Number** as the data type for this field.

Puzzled?

The Byte option for Field Size enables you to enter any positive, whole number between 0 and 255. For help using the Field Size property, press the F1 Key.

3 Press **F6**, or click the Field Size text box, and click the arrow button to display the drop-down list box. Select the **Byte** option.

Missing Link

For number fields, the Field Size property enables you to choose the type of number. The range of numbers which you can enter in this field is determined by the choice you make for the Field Size.

Puzzled? Notes

You may find that you performed a task, such as sorting data, that you didn't want to do after all. The Puzzled? notes tell you how to undo certain procedures or get out of a situation such as displaying a Help screen.

Missing Link

Many tasks contain other short notes that tell you a little more about certain procedures. These notes define terms, explain other options, refer you to other sections when applicable, and so on.

19

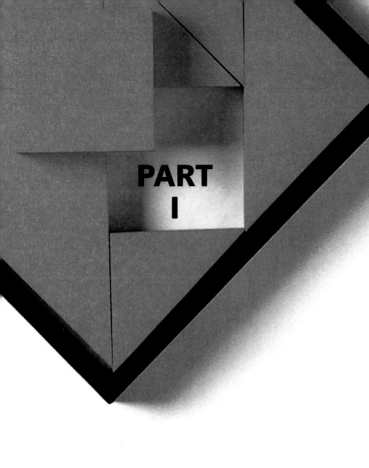

PART I

Learning the Basics

1 Installing Access

2 Starting Access from the Start Button

3 Opening an Existing Database

4 Using Menu Commands

5 Using Toolbar Buttons and Tabs

6 Getting Help

7 Using Context-Sensitive Help

8 Using the Office Assistant

9 Exiting Access

10 Creating a Shortcut for Access on Your Desktop

▲ ● ■ ▲ ● ■ ▲ ●

P ART I INTRODUCES YOU TO MICROSOFT ACCESS 97 for Windows (referred to as *Access* throughout the rest of this book) by showing you how to start the program and how to use the menu and toolbars. Throughout the tasks in this book, you will learn the easiest way to perform each operation, usually with the mouse.

There are a few simple database concepts and terms that you should know before you continue with *Easy Microsoft Access 97*. A database consists of one or more *tables*. A table stores information about a specific item or thing; customers, orders, products, suppliers, etc. in rows and columns. The information contained in a table shouldn't be able to be subdivided into two different categories, such as customers and their orders. (These two subjects can be divided into customers, order information, items ordered, and inventory).

Each row of a table is a single *record*. The record contains all of the information about a single entry in the table. One record may contain a customer's name, address, telephone number, credit limit, and customer identification number. Another table may contain records about products: the product's ID, name, description, cost, selling price as well as the quantity on hand, the quantity on order, and the supplier ID.

Each column of the table is commonly called a *field*. A field is the smallest distinct piece of information a record will contain. In a customer table, for example, you may have individual fields for: customer ID number, customer last name, customer first name, street, city, state, country, zip/postal code, and telephone number. The information in a field shouldn't be further divisible into logical fields. For example, a customer name field containing both first and last names can easily be divided into two fields: first name and last name fields. This is a logical division and so you should create a field for each. On the other hand, you would not (under most circumstances) divide a street field into one field for street number and another for street name—because it is not a logical division.

When you create a database, it is usually composed of several tables which are related to each other in some meaningful way. Each table contains a specific type of data for the entire database. One table may contain information about customers; another table holds information about orders; and a third table has information about the products that you sell. You use *queries*, *forms*, and *reports* to combine and join information from each table. Tables, queries, forms, and reports are all types of Access *objects*. Within Access, you store and manipulate your information through these and other objects. You will become familiar with each of these objects and many others in the various tasks of this book.

In this part of *Easy Microsoft Access 97*, you will learn to open an Access database file, to select menu commands, and to use the Toolbar. This part also covers the Help system and the new Office Assistant. If you are already familiar with Windows 95 (you know how to open and exit programs and use Windows 95 style menus), you may want to skip ahead to Task 6 and the coverage of the new Help systems. If Windows 95 is unfamiliar to you, be sure to thoroughly read and work through each task. Many of the basic features that you will learn here are applicable to numerous Windows 95 applications. Access will also run under Microsoft Windows NT 3.51 and 4.0.

Although you can utilize most Access features using either the mouse or the keyboard, many functions are easier when you use the mouse, and some are accessible *only* with a mouse. At this writing you can input information into a field only with the keyboard; the keyboard will remain the sole input method until mice learn to type or until voice input becomes a reality.

TASK 1

Installing Access

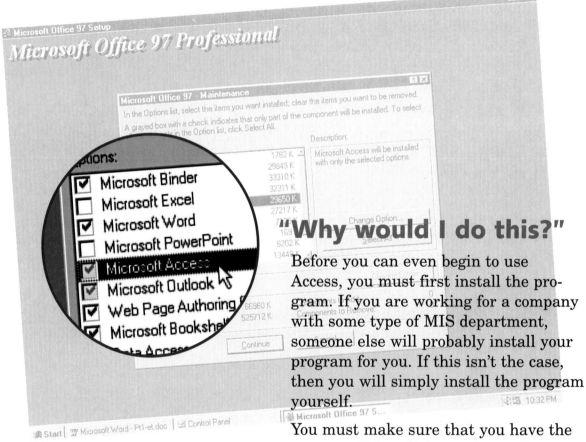

"Why would I do this?"

Before you can even begin to use Access, you must first install the program. If you are working for a company with some type of MIS department, someone else will probably install your program for you. If this isn't the case, then you will simply install the program yourself.

You must make sure that you have the program CD or disks, and your license or CD key number handy, as this task will work from the assumption that you have purchased Microsoft Office Professional and are installing the program from a CD. The process is similar if you are using the disk format, except that you will have to feed your computer disks when on-screen directions ask you to do so.

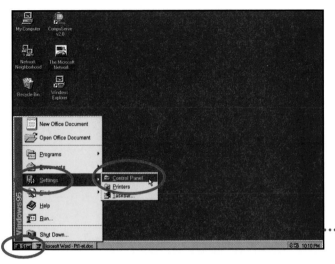

1 Place the Microsoft Office Professional CD in your computer CD drive. Click the **Start** button on the Windows task bar, and choose the **Settings** option. Choose the **Control Panel** option from the submenu displayed.

2 From the Control Panel window now displayed on your screen, select and start the **Add/Remove Programs** option by double-clicking it with your left mouse button.

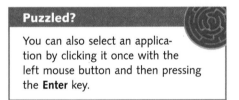

Puzzled?

You can also select an application by clicking it once with the left mouse button and then pressing the **Enter** key.

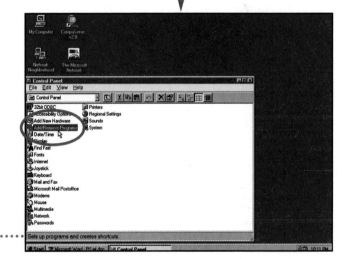

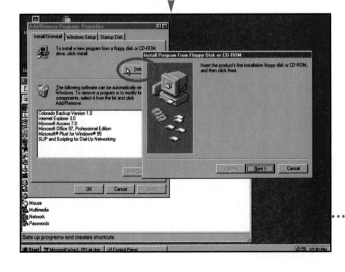

3 Click the **Install** button in the Add/Remove Programs Properties dialog box to start the Program Install Wizard. This Wizard will help you to begin the installation process.

4 Click the **Next >** button on the Wizard dialog box. If the Wizard has found your CD drive, the file SETUP.EXE should now be displayed in the text box. Click the **Finish** button. The installation program SETUP will start.

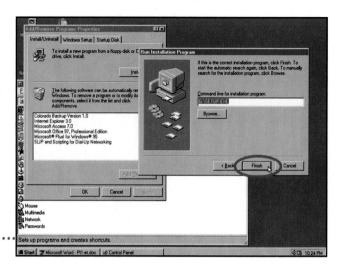

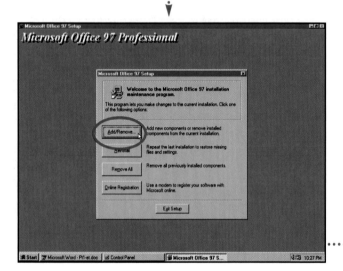

5 When Setup has finished searching for previously installed versions of Microsoft Office, you'll see the Welcome dialog box. Click the **Add/Remove** button to install or remove a component of Microsoft Office Professional.

6 Be sure that the check box beside Microsoft Access has a check mark inside it (if not click the check box). This will ensure that Microsoft Access will be installed. Click the **Continue** button.

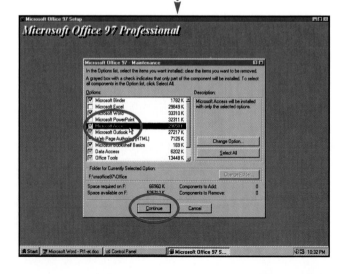

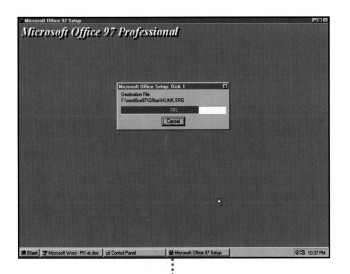

7 You will see a status dialog box telling you what files are being installed and the percentage of the process that has been completed. Now a new dialog box telling you that Microsoft Office Professional has been installed is displayed. Click the **OK** button.

Missing Link

If you want all of the normal components of the program to be installed, leave all of the default settings as they are.

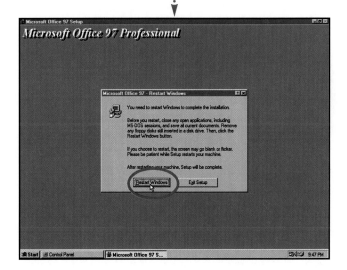

8 You must now allow Setup to reboot your computer so that all of the changes it has made will take effect. Click the **Restart Windows** button. Microsoft Office Professional will be ready for your use when Windows starts again. ■

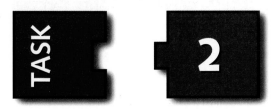

Starting Access from the Start Button

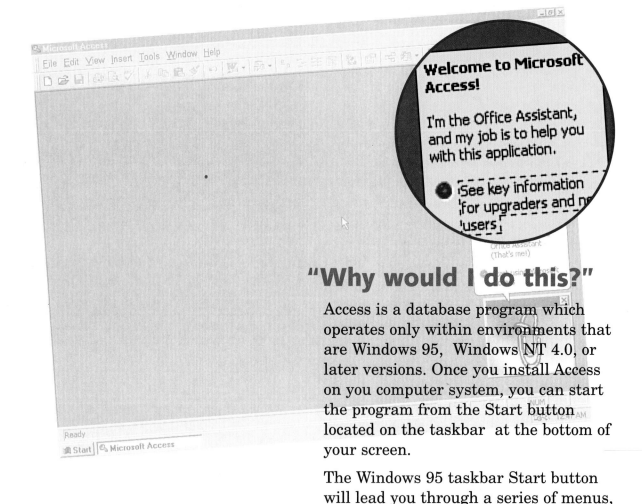

Welcome to Microsoft Access!

I'm the Office Assistant, and my job is to help you with this application.

● See key information for upgraders and new users

"Why would I do this?"

Access is a database program which operates only within environments that are Windows 95, Windows NT 4.0, or later versions. Once you install Access on you computer system, you can start the program from the Start button located on the taskbar at the bottom of your screen.

The Windows 95 taskbar Start button will lead you through a series of menus, enabling you to open and work with the various applications that have been installed on your computer. In this task, you will learn to use the Start button to open Access.

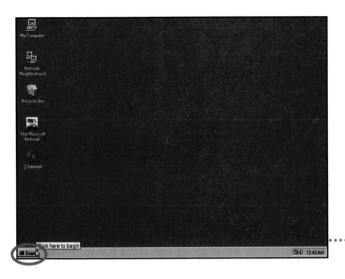

1 Place the mouse pointer on the Start button located in the left-hand corner of your screen on the taskbar. When you hold the mouse still on the button, you will see the tooltip, Click here to begin floating above the Start button.

2 Click the left button on your mouse to access the first Start button menu.

Puzzled?

You can select the Start button by pressing and holding the **Ctrl** key while you press the **Esc** key. Then release both keys together. When the Start menu appears, menu options can be selected by using the up and down arrow keys to move the selector bar.

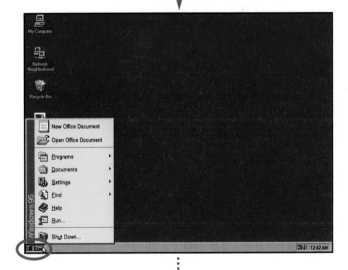

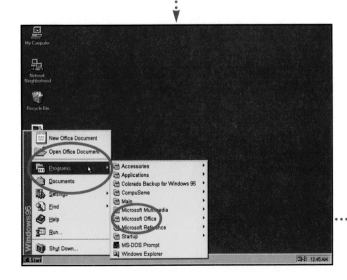

3 Move the mouse pointer up to the Programs menu option. You will see the Programs submenu displayed to the right of the primary menu list.

Task 2: Starting Access from the Start Button

4 Move your mouse pointer across to the Programs submenu and select Microsoft Office option, again displaying another submenu. Click on the Microsoft Access option to start the program.

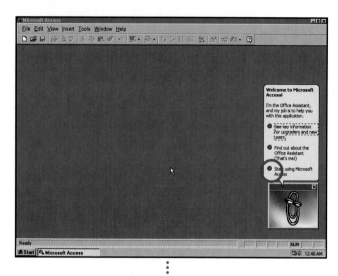

Missing Link

Your Start menu system may be slightly different, and it may not have a Microsoft Office option. Look for Microsoft Access, Access 97, Office, or Applications on the Start menu.

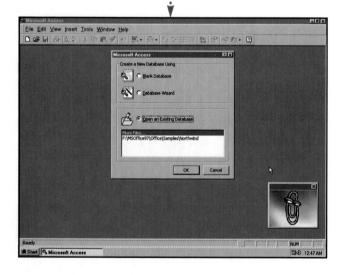

5 Click the Start Using Microsoft Access button on the Office Assistant's balloon. ■

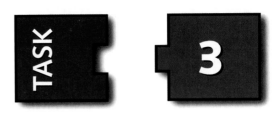

Opening an Existing Database

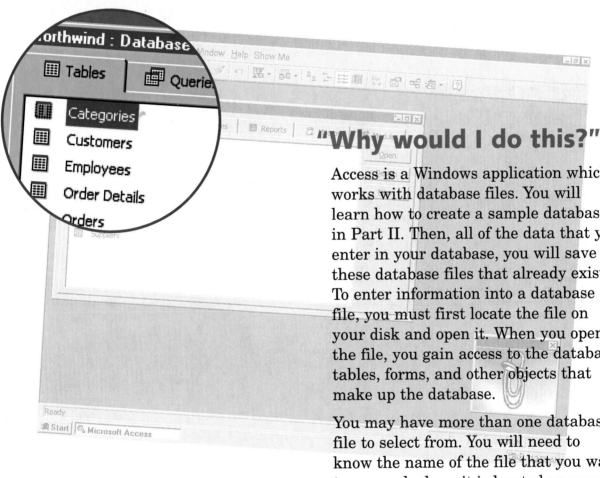

"Why would I do this?"

Access is a Windows application which works with database files. You will learn how to create a sample database in Part II. Then, all of the data that you enter in your database, you will save in these database files that already exist. To enter information into a database file, you must first locate the file on your disk and open it. When you open the file, you gain access to the database tables, forms, and other objects that make up the database.

You may have more than one database file to select from. You will need to know the name of the file that you want to use and where it is located on your disk. In this task, you will learn to select a database file and then open it. The sample database provided with Access, Northwind Traders, will be used for this task. It is installed along with the program.

Task 3: Opening an Existing Database

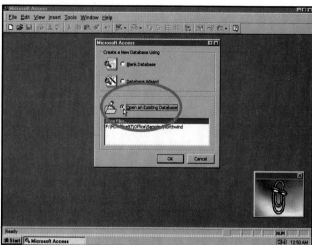

1 Once you start Access, this dialog box appears. Select the option button **Open an Existing Database** by clicking on the option button circle once. A black dot will appear in the option button which means that it is selected.

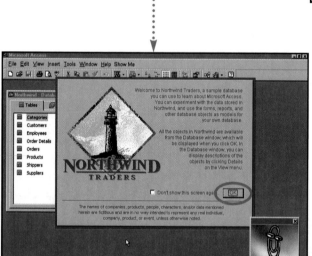

2 Move the mouse pointer to the **Northwind** option in the list box and click the **OK** button. Click the **OK** button on the opening form to close it. ■

Missing Link

If you accidentally open a different database, simply clicking the **Close** button (the button with the **X** on it) at the upper-right corner of the Database window will close it. But make sure you click the correct Close button—if you click the Close button on the Access window, the application will close and you will have to start Access again.

Using Menu Commands

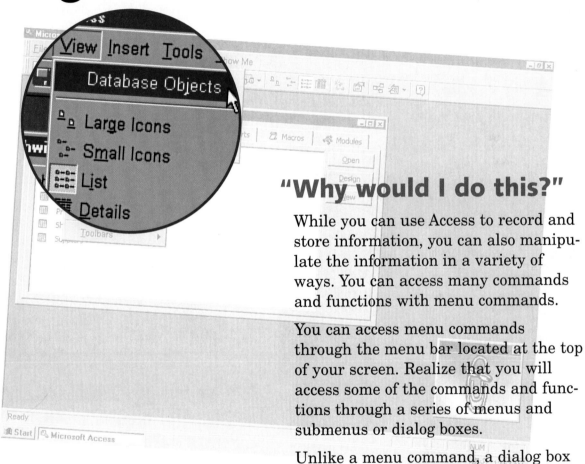

"Why would I do this?"

While you can use Access to record and store information, you can also manipulate the information in a variety of ways. You can access many commands and functions with menu commands.

You can access menu commands through the menu bar located at the top of your screen. Realize that you will access some of the commands and functions through a series of menus and submenus or dialog boxes.

Unlike a menu command, a dialog box allows you to make several choices about the object that you are working with, and then apply all of the choices you've made at one time. You can select menu commands and many options available in dialog boxes by using either the keyboard or the mouse. When available, key combinations will display to the right of the command on the menu.

Task 4: Using Menu Commands

1 Move your mouse pointer to the **Edit** menu command on the menu bar and click the left mouse button. You will see the Edit drop-down menu display.

Missing Link

Notice that some menu options have a two-key combination to their right. You can access these menu options without going through the menus by pressing the **Ctrl** key and the indicated letter at the same time. Menu items which are dimmed are not available.

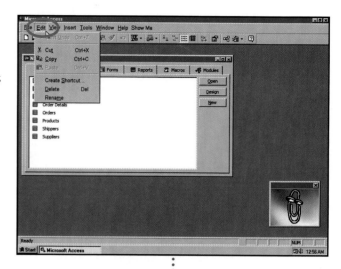

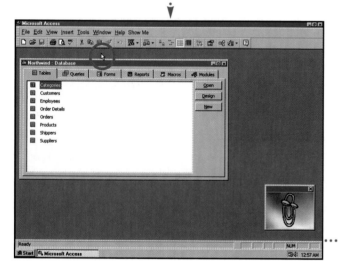

2 Move the mouse pointer to a blank area on the Access desktop, away from the menu bar and the drop-down menu; click once to deselect both objects.

3 Press the **Alt** key on your keyboard to activate the menu. Press the **V** to display the View drop-down menu.

Missing Link

Any time that you see an underlined letter on a menu option it is called a *hot key*. You can use the hot key by holding down both the **Alt** key and the underlined letter on your keyboard.

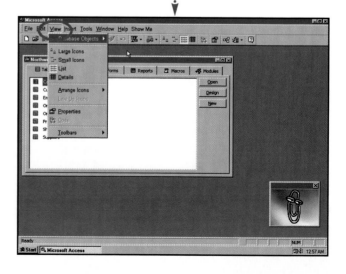

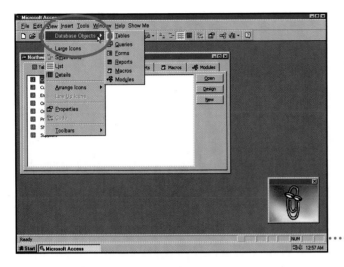

4 Choose the **Database Objects** option from the View menu by clicking it once. You will see a submenu displayed on the right which lists the six Access object groups. The current object is indicated by the depressed button beside its name, in this case Tables.

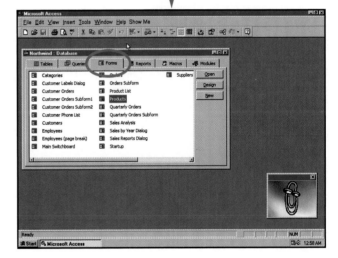

5 Select the **Forms** object from the submenu. You will see the Database window change from the Tables group to the Forms group. ■

TASK 5

Using Toolbar Buttons and Tabs

"Why would I do this?"

Many commands and functions are only a single mouse click away when you use the toolbars which are available to you. Not all commands are available on a toolbar, just as not all toolbar features are represented on the menus. As you work with different objects in Access, the toolbar will automatically change, adding and removing features not applicable to the object you are working with. Depending on the object you are currently working with, Access may add secondary toolbars to your screen with additional functions. You can display more than a single toolbar at a time, and toolbars can be moved on your screen.

While you can customize a toolbar, adding or removing buttons from one of the standard toolbars, or from your own toolbar design, these options are beyond the scope of Easy Access 97.

At the top of the Database window is a series of six tab buttons. These are used to gain access to the major object categories: tables, queries, forms, reports, macros, and modules. You must use the mouse to work with tab buttons and toolbars.

22

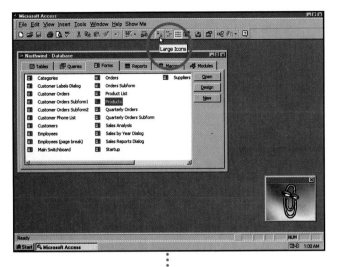

1 To use any of the functions available on the toolbar, place the mouse pointer on it.

Puzzled?

When you pause the mouse pointer on a toolbar button a ScreenTip is displayed. A ScreenTip is a brief description of a button. ScreenTips can be turned on or off from the Toolbars Customize dialog box. Select **View**, **Toolbars**, **Customize** from the menu, or right-click the mouse on the toolbar to open this dialog box.

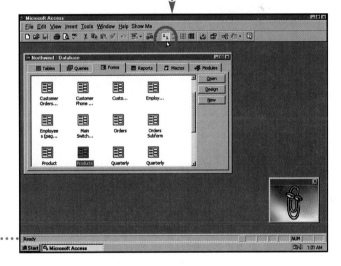

2 Click the left mouse button once to activate the function for the selected toolbar button. In this example, you will see the various options listed in the Form's box now displayed with large icons. Select each toolbar buttons this way.

3 The tab buttons on the Database window can be used to access any of the six primary groups of Access objects. Move the mouse pointer to the **Tables** tab button.

Task 5: Using Toolbar Buttons and Tabs

4 Click the left mouse button. You will see the Database window shift from the Forms list to the Tables list. Notice that the tables are displayed with large icons.

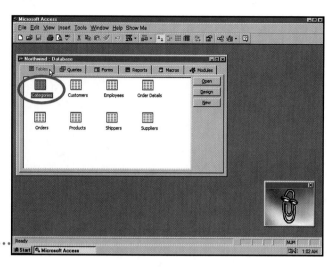

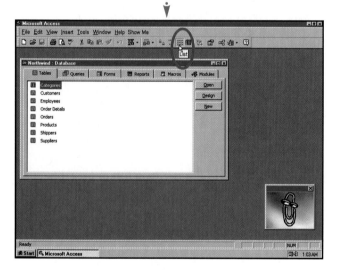

5 Move the mouse pointer to the **List** button on the toolbar and click it once. You will see the table display revert to its original order and icon size. ■

Puzzled?

Just select another tab button if you accidentally click on the wrong one. Notice how the tab's text changes color as you move the mouse over it. The tab with the blue text is the one which will be selected when clicked.

Getting Help

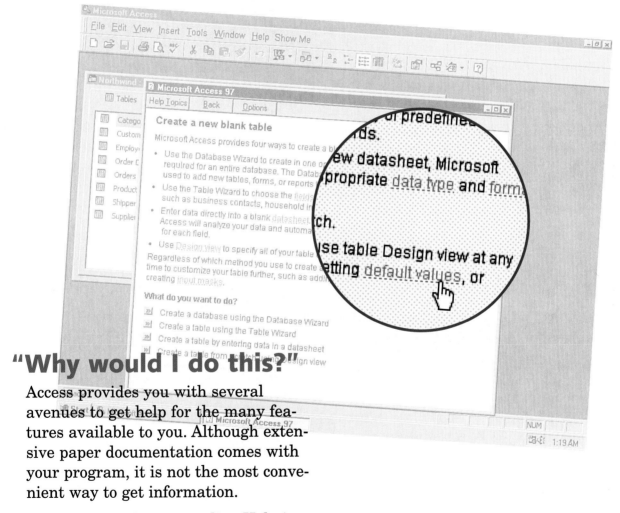

"Why would I do this?"

Access provides you with several avenues to get help for the many features available to you. Although extensive paper documentation comes with your program, it is not the most convenient way to get information.

Access' comprehensive online Help is a very easy way to find out what a feature or command is used for. From within the Access Help system, you can choose from three major venues: a table of contents, an index, and a find system.

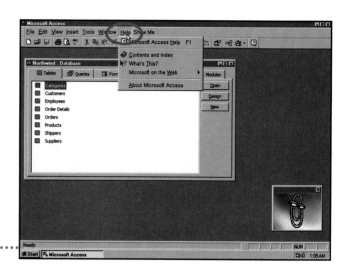

1 Move the mouse pointer to the **Help** menu command on the menu bar and click the left mouse button. This displays the Help menu with a list of available options.

2 Select **Contents and Index**. You will see the Help Topics dialog box. This screen has three tabs: Contents, Index, and Find. If it's not, click the Contents tab to bring it to the front. Each of these tab options provides help in a different format.

Missing Link

By clicking on one of the Contents tab's book icons, you can view additional subtopics and details about the selected subject. Double-click the book icon to collapse all the subtopics.

3 Double-click the book icon for `Introduction to Microsoft Access 97`. You will see the icon change to an open book icon, with a list of subtopics displayed below it.

Missing Link

If a subtopic appears with a closed book icon, then it too has additional subtopics. If a page with a ? on it appears, an explanation of a particular help topic will display when you click the icon.

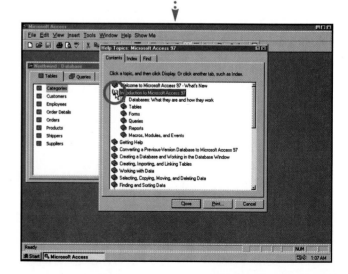

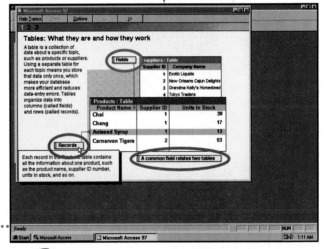

4 Double-click the subtopic icon **Tables**, and then on the topic icon **Tables: What they are and how they work** to view the information about this topic. The screen which appears displays information about the selected topic, and often enables you to choose additional pages of information.

5 Move the mouse pointer over each of the three callouts labeled: Fields, Records, and A common field relates two tables. The pointer changes from an arrow to a hand with a pointing finger. Click one of these callouts to display a definition box. Click the mouse anywhere on the window to remove the definition box.

6 Move the mouse pointer to the number **2** underneath the menu and click it once. Click the number **3** to display the third and final screen.

Puzzled?

Whenever you see text in a help box displayed in a green font with a dashed line under the text, clicking it will display a definition for the term, while clicking green text under-lined in solid green will send you to a new help screen. This assumes you are using standard color settings.

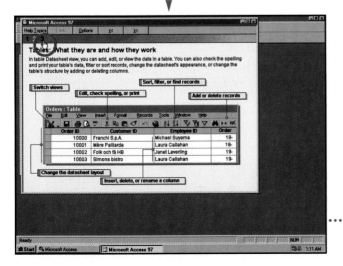

7 Click the **Help Topics** button to return to the main help dialog box. Click the **Index** tab to display the Index dialog box.

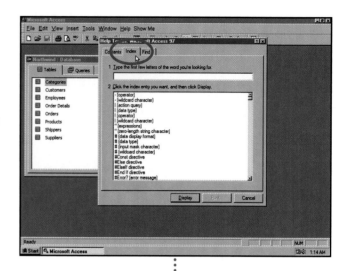

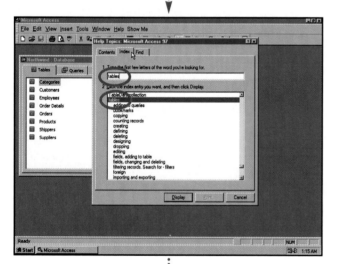

8 To view help on specific topics, type a word or phrase into the first text box at the top of the dialog box. For instance, type **tables** into the text box. You will see a list of all Help Topics beginning with the word "tables" displayed in the second list box.

9 To view the help available for one of the topics listed, click on **creating**. Notice how your entry in the text box changes to match what you have selected. You can use the horizontal scroll bar to view additional Help Topics.

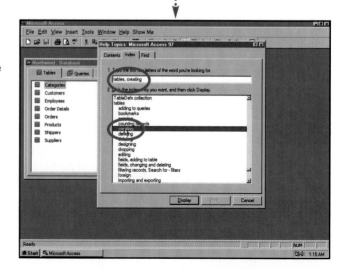

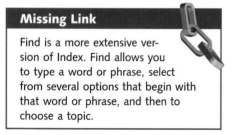

Missing Link

Find is a more extensive version of Index. Find allows you to type a word or phrase, select from several options that begin with that word or phrase, and then to choose a topic.

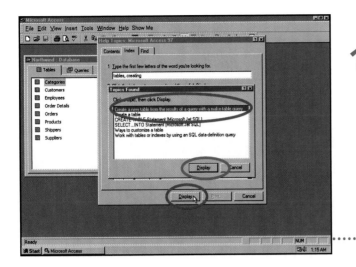

10 Click the **Display** button. Depending on the particular help you have selected, you will now see a secondary dialog box called Topics Found, or the actual help text. If your help has displayed the Topics Found dialog box, select the topic which most closely represents the topic you want, then click the **Display** button.

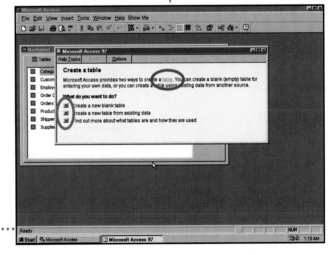

11 Select the second option **Create a table** from the Topics Found dialog box, and click the **Display** button. The help dialog box now displayed has three types of help: text, the green jump text to display a definition pop-up, and three buttons which when clicked will display more help screens.

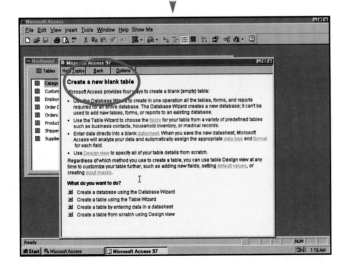

12 Click on the **Create a new blank table** button. This screen will show you help more specific to the subject of creating a new table, and give you more options to see definitions, and buttons to go on to more help screens. Click on the **Close** (**X**) button at the upper-right corner of the help dialog box to close it. ■

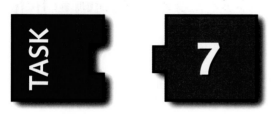

Using Context-Sensitive Help

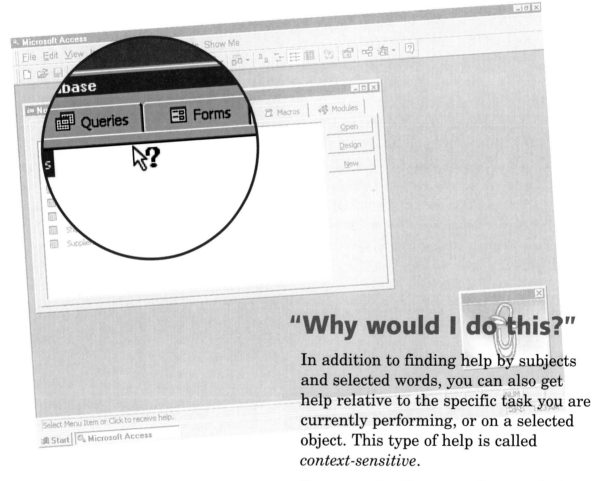

"Why would I do this?"

In addition to finding help by subjects and selected words, you can also get help relative to the specific task you are currently performing, or on a selected object. This type of help is called *context-sensitive*.

For example, if you aren't sure what a specific object does, or you simply want a better definition than a ScreenTip, using the context-sensitive help option will display a pop-up definition of the selected object.

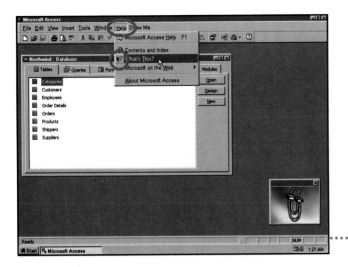

1 Select the **Help** menu on the menu bar, then click the **What's This?** option from the drop-down menu list.

2 The mouse pointer changes shape to an arrow with a question mark.

Missing Link

You can also display the What's This mouse pointer by pressing **Shift+F1** from the keyboard.

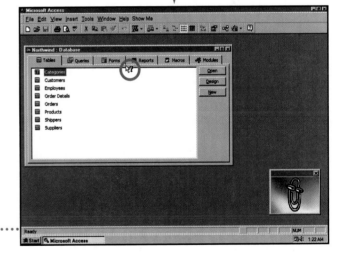

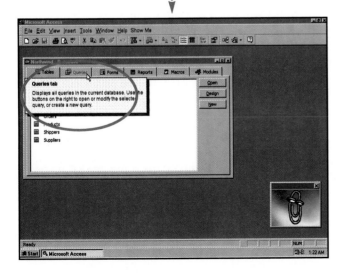

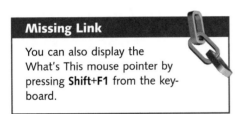

3 Move the mouse pointer to the **Queries** tab and click it. You will now see a pop-up definition box for the Queries tab. Click the mouse anywhere on the Access Desktop to remove the definition box. The mouse pointer automatically returns to its normal shape and function. ■

Using the Office Assistant

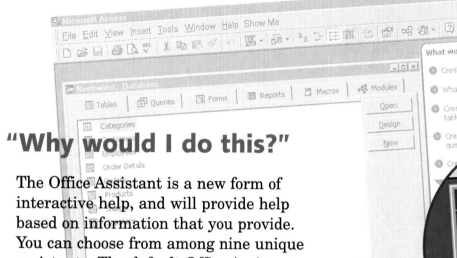

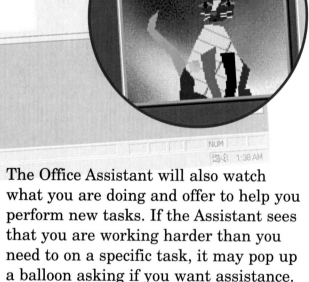

"Why would I do this?"

The Office Assistant is a new form of interactive help, and will provide help based on information that you provide. You can choose from among nine unique assistants. The default Office Assistant is named "Clippit" and looks like an animated paper clip. Clippit will appear on your screen when you start Access for the first time. Use the one which best fits with your personality. You can set many different options for your assistant; they can make sounds, or be animated; they can be activated when you press the F1 key.

If you need help, you can click on the Office Assistant and type a question into the place provided in the dialog balloon. The Office Assistant will then search for, and display, several topics that may help you answer your question.

The Office Assistant will also watch what you are doing and offer to help you perform new tasks. If the Assistant sees that you are working harder than you need to on a specific task, it may pop up a balloon asking if you want assistance.

The Office Assistant can also show daily tips. These tips change each time that you start Access, or you can view and cycle through them.

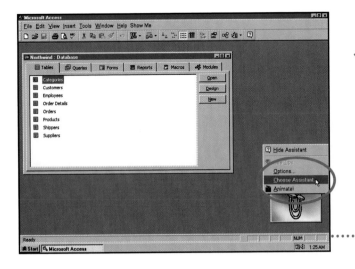

1 The default office assistant is Clippit who appears as an animated paper clip. You can begin the selection of a new assistant by placing the mouse pointer on Clippit and clicking the right mouse button. Select the **Choose Assistant** option on the pop-up menu. The Office Assistant dialog box will now be displayed.

2 Click the **Next >** button to cycle through each of the remaining office assistants.

Missing Link

Changing the Office Assistant takes just a few mouse clicks and does not affect any other aspect of your database. This is determined by simple personal preference.

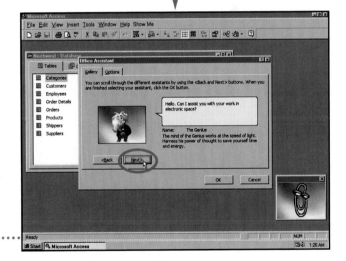

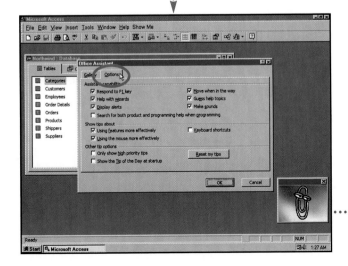

3 As each is displayed, they will display some of their animation features for you. Once you have decided upon the assistant that you want to use, move the mouse pointer to the **Options** tab and click it.

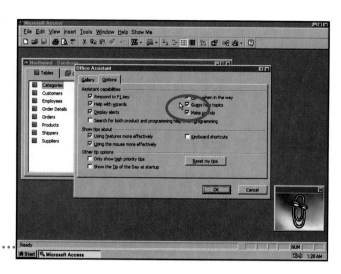

4 The assistant options include three groups of check boxes. When a check box is selected, the option is turned on. If an option has been checked, you can click it with the mouse pointer to turn the option off.

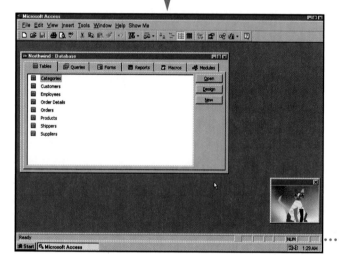

5 Click the **OK** button to save your selection of an assistant and any option changes you may have made.

6 Click on the assistant's window. You will see a balloon appear which contains several buttons and a text box.

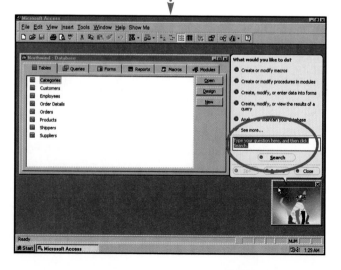

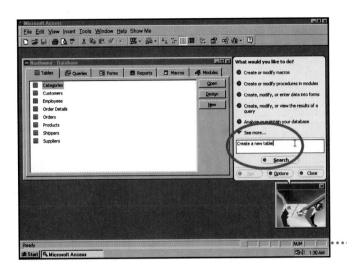

7 Type a word or phrase in the text box for a topic on which you want more information.

8 Click the **Search** button. You will now see a new balloon with several topic options. In our example, you see Scribbles thinking about the topic to be found.

Puzzled?

If none of these topics seem to provide the help that you are looking for, click on the **See more** option to view more help topics. You can also try rewording your request and then click the **Search** button again.

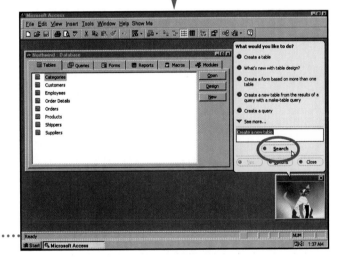

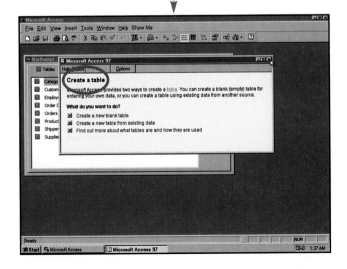

9 Click the button beside the option **Create a table**. You will see a help dialog box displayed for this topic. From here you can read this screen, go on to other screens by clicking the other buttons, or close the screen by clicking the **Close** (**X**) button at the upper-right corner. ■

Exiting Access

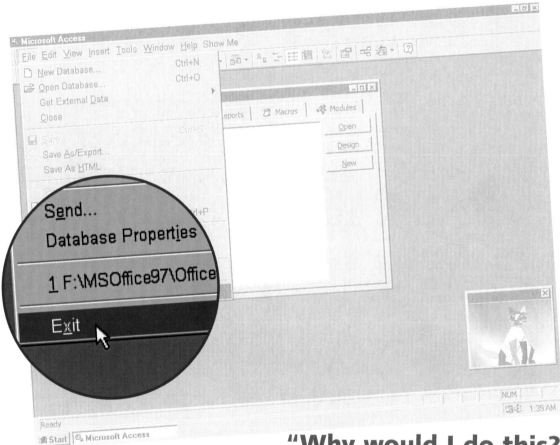

"Why would I do this?"

Once you have completed your tasks in Access, or any time you leave your computer for a length of time, or at the end of the day, you should properly exit from the program. In the event of a power or hardware failure, this will increase your chances of a successful information recovery.

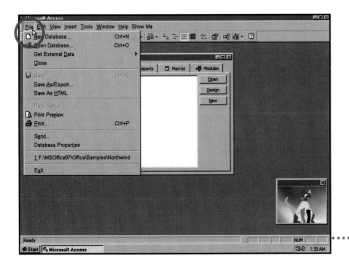

1 Open the **File** menu, displaying the File drop-down menu list.

Puzzled?

You can also exit from Access by clicking the **Close** button (**X**) in the upper-right corner of the program window, or by pressing the **Alt+F4** key combination.

2 Click the **Exit** command on the File menu. The Access program window closes. Part II will show you how to save your database files. ■

Missing Link

If you select the File menu option and then decide that you are not ready to exit from the Access program, simply press the **Esc** key to back out of the menu. You can also click the mouse anywhere on the desktop to close the menu.

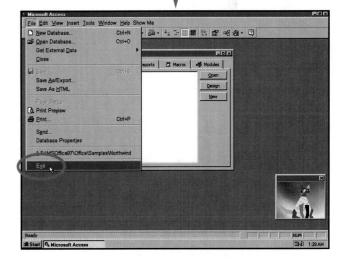

Creating a Shortcut for Access on Your Desktop

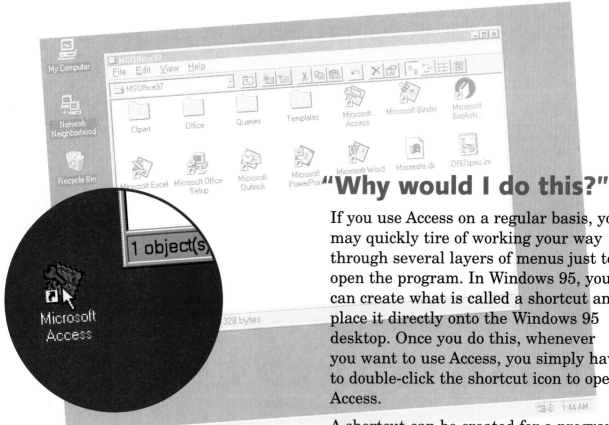

"Why would I do this?"

If you use Access on a regular basis, you may quickly tire of working your way through several layers of menus just to open the program. In Windows 95, you can create what is called a shortcut and place it directly onto the Windows 95 desktop. Once you do this, whenever you want to use Access, you simply have to double-click the shortcut icon to open Access.

A shortcut can be created for a program, such as Access, or for a database file. When you create a shortcut for a database, it does two things: first it launches the Access program, and then loads the database. This enables you to quickly (in just two mouse clicks) do what would otherwise take you several seconds and many mouse clicks to do.

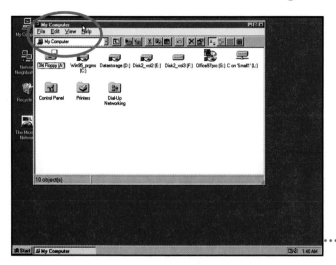

1 Double-click the icon labeled **My Computer** on your Windows 95 desktop. You will see a window that displays an icon for each of the drives that you have on your computer as well as a Control Panel and Printers icon. You may or may not have other icons, depending on whether you are connected to a network.

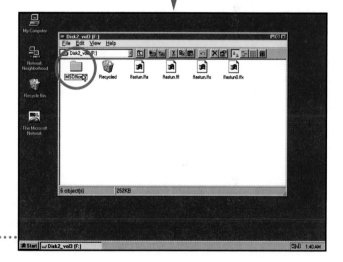

2 Select the icon for the drive where you have the Access program stored, and double-click it. For most of you this drive icon will be labeled (C:). (On my computer, Access is stored under my F: drive.) A new window will be displayed showing folders from the selected drive.

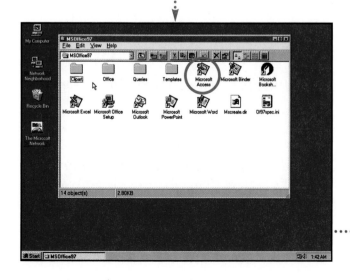

3 Choose and double-click the folder which contains the Access program or folder. In this example, it is the MSOffice97 folder. The MSOffice97 window now appears with its folders.

> **Missing Link**
>
> If you don't find the file or folder from memory, you can always use the Windows Explorer to help you to find the Access program file.

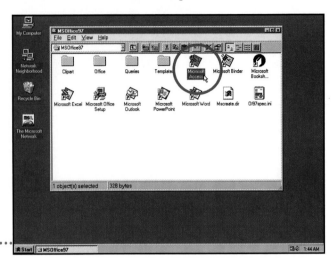

4 The icon for the Access program is represented by a gold key on a form, and is labeled Microsoft Access. Use the horizontal scroll bar to scroll through the folder until you find the file you are looking for. Select this file by clicking it once.

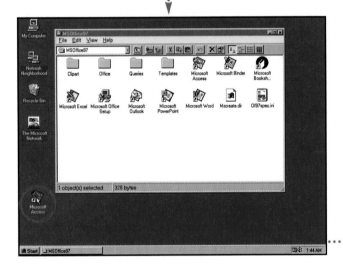

5 Drag the Access icon from the window and drop it on the blank space above the Start button. Drop it by letting the mouse button go.

6 You will now see a new icon labeled Shortcut to Microsoft Access. Close any folder windows that may be open by clicking their **Close (X)** buttons. ■

Missing Link

The next time that you are ready to start Access, simply double-click this shortcut icon. The small arrow in the lower-left corner of the icon indicates that it is a shortcut.

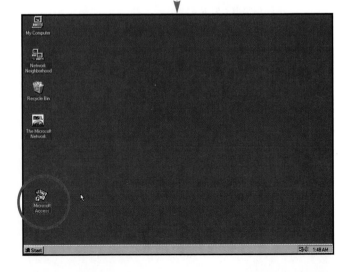

PART II

Designing and Creating an Access Database

11 Creating a New Database

12 Using the Table Wizard

13 Adding a New Field in Design View

14 Working with Numbers

15 Using a Yes/No Field

16 Saving the New Table Definition

17 Opening a Table

18 Changing a Field Name

19 Moving a Field Within a Table

20 Inserting a Field

21 Adding a New Field in Datasheet View

22 Deleting a Field

23 Building a Table from Scratch

T HIS PART INTRODUCES YOU TO THE ESSENTIAL ELEMENTS that go into designing and creating a table.

A table contains all the information about a specific subject. Each row of the table contains an individual *record*. Every record in a table is unique—there is no record in the table that is a duplicate of any other record in the table. This is one of the greatest powers of a *relational database management system* such as Access, ensuring that all records in a table are unique. In the case of a customer table, each record holds all of the information about one of your customers.

Each record is made up of elements called *fields*. Each field describes a unique piece of information in the record. In the case of the Customer table there may be fields for: Customer ID, Company Name, Address, City, State, and Zip/Postal Code.

You can format a field to control the type of information which it will contain. For example, you can format the Quantity field in the Line Items table to accept only numbers. This prevents you from accidentally entering ABC into this field. You can also format a field to accept only valid dates, or text of a specified length.

The goal of a relational database such as Access is to remove the need for duplicated information. In a relational database, a table holds only a specific type of information. Information in one table is then *related* (using a unique identification field) to the information contained in another table. If for some reason you need to edit data, such as a customer's address, you only have to make your changes in one table.

The table demonstrates how a relational database works. It shows four database tables that each contain information about a specific subject. The tables are then related through a specific identifier, or *foreign key*. For example, the Customer table is related to the Invoice table because each invoice is identified with a customer through the Customer ID field. When tables are related in this way, each customer must have their own unique Customer ID, otherwise you can have an invoice that may be linked to more than one customer.

Most tables that you create in Access use a *primary key* field as a unique identifying field. A primary key field by definition cannot have a duplicate value anywhere in the table. The easiest way to link two tables together is to use the primary key field of one table as a *foreign key* in the second table. A foreign key field must be related to its primary key counterpart. These fields can be related if they use the same (or compatible) data type. The Customer table in our example uses the Customer ID field as its primary key, while the Invoice table uses this same field as a foreign key to create a relationship between the tables.

Customer	Invoice	Line Items	Inventory
Customer ID	Invoice Number	Invoice Number	Item Code
Company Name	Customer ID	Item Code	Item Description
Address City	Invoice Date Ordered	Unit Price Quantity Hand	Supplier Quantity On
State			Unit Cost
Zip/Postal Code			

The table in our example contains information fields such as Company Name, Address, Invoice Number, Invoice Date, Item Sold, and Price. Each of these tables contains a field that provides a unique identifying value for each record in that table. This field provides a link to at least one other table. The arrows indicate the linking fields between the four tables.

Dividing your information into groups or subjects allows you to condense the sheer quantity of information to a much smaller fraction of what a single table requires. Division also helps to ensure that the information is not duplicated and that it is more accurate.

Creating a New Database

"Why would I do this?"

Before you can begin to build any of the objects which make up your database, you must create the file that holds the objects (tables, reports, queries, and so on). The database file is the container in which your information will reside.

When creating your database file you'll need to place it in a folder on your disk. You may want to place the database in an existing folder (by default, all files are saved to the My Documents folder) or you can create a new folder and name it something that will help you remember the files it contains. You'll need to give the file a unique, meaningful name that will help you remember

the contents. Access automatically names your database *db1*. Unless you plan to create only a single database file, you will want to provide your database files with more descriptive names.

You are no longer limited to the old style, eight-character document name, so use a descriptive name for the database. A database name can be a maximum of 64 characters and can include spaces and most other characters. A name can't begin with a space, and it can't contain periods, exclamation points, or a back quote character.

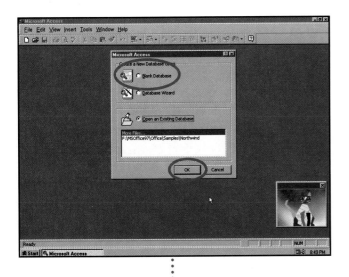

1 Double-click the Access shortcut icon that you just created in Task 10. The program starts.

> **Puzzled?**
>
> If Access is already open, you can create a new database file by selecting **File**, **New Database** from the menu, or by using the keyboard shortcut **Ctrl+N**.

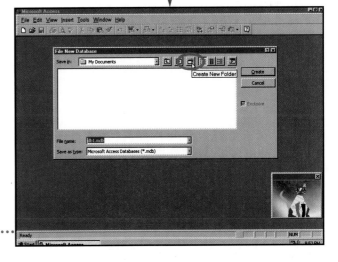

2 Click the **Blank Database** option button, and then the **OK** button. The File New Database dialog box is displayed. To create a new folder to store your file, first, use the Save In: drop down list to locate the disk and folder in which you want this new folder to reside. Click the Create New Folder icon.

3 In the Name text box, type the name of your file. In our example, we've chosen the name Plant Files.

Task 11: Creating a New Database

4 Click **OK**. In our example, the Plant Files folder is a subfolder of the My Documents folder.

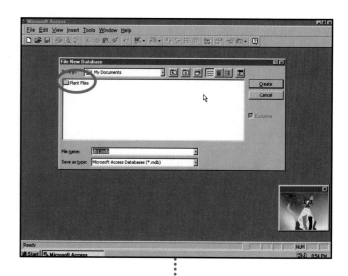

Missing Link

By creating subfolders, you can group together the documents that you use frequently. You can always move a document to a different folder later if the one you originally use is not convenient.

5 Double-click the **Plant Files** folder to select it. In the File name text box, as the name for your new database document follow along with our example, and type **Garden Plants**. Access will automatically append the file extension, mdb, onto the database's name.

Puzzled?

Documents and files are similar terms. Windows 95 uses a folder and document metaphor for the older terms of "path" and "file."

6 Click the **Create** button. The database file Garden Plants is created and placed in the folder Plant Files. Open the new database. All of the object windows that now appear in the Database window will be blank because this is a new database. ■

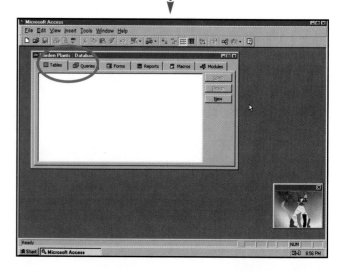

Using the Table Wizard

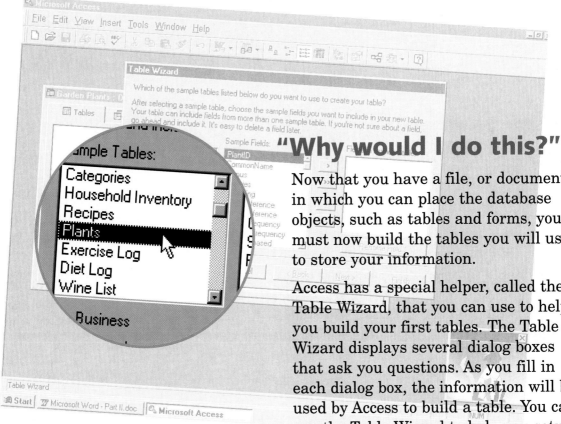

"Why would I do this?"

Now that you have a file, or document in which you can place the database objects, such as tables and forms, you must now build the tables you will use to store your information.

Access has a special helper, called the Table Wizard, that you can use to help you build your first tables. The Table Wizard displays several dialog boxes that ask you questions. As you fill in each dialog box, the information will be used by Access to build a table. You can use the Table Wizard to help you setup a complete or partial database table. You have a choice of 25 Business categories, and 20 Personal categories.

As mentioned in the introduction to this part, spend some time designing your database on paper before you begin this task. This will save you a lot of rework later on, when you could discover that you can't find the information you need.

1 Before you can add a table to a database, it must first be opened. If the database Garden Plants is not open, then click the **Open Database** button on the toolbar, and select the document **Garden Plants** from the **Plant Files** folder. Finally, click the **Open** button on the dialog box.

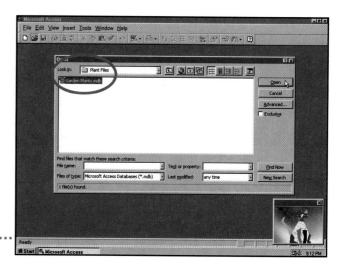

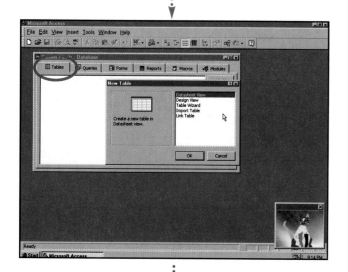

2 Be sure that the Tables tab is active, by clicking it. Now click the **New** button on the Database window. It is currently the only active button available to you on the Database window at this time. This will open the New Table dialog box.

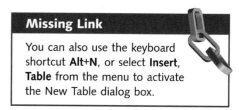

Missing Link

You can also use the keyboard shortcut **Alt+N**, or select **Insert**, **Table** from the menu to activate the New Table dialog box.

3 Select the **Table Wizard** option from the list box and then click the **OK** button.

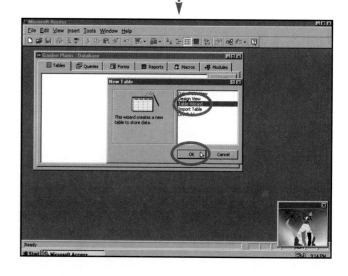

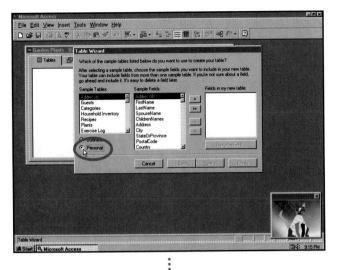

4 Click the **Personal** option button. Access displays the personal category of tables in the Sample Tables list box.

Missing Link

To view the various options for pre-defined tables, scroll up and down both the Business and Personal lists. The Sample Fields list box displays the list of field names you can use in the predefined table you have selected in the Sample Tables list box.

5 Scroll down the Sample Tables list box until you see the table name **Plants**. Select it by clicking the name once. You will now see a new list of predefined fields in the Sample Fields list box.

Puzzled?

If you do not see a field in the Sample Fields list box for a specific type of information that you want to collect, you can add this field to the table definition later. For more information, see Task 13 "Adding a New Field in Design View."

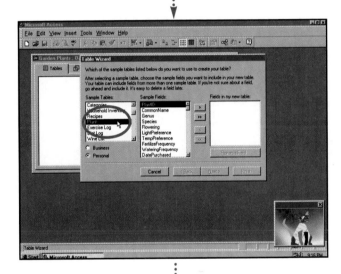

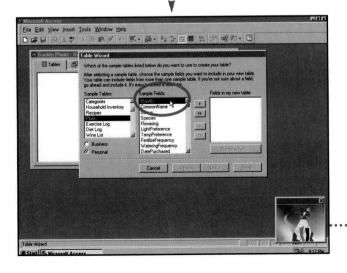

6 Click the **PlantID** field in the Sample Fields list box to select it. This is the first field that you will include in the new table. When you select a field from the list box, Access highlights it.

Missing Link

When you select and add a field from the Sample Fields list to your table, you add the field name and all of the pre-defined formatting information for that field.

7 Click the > button. Access copies the selected field name to the Fields in my new table list box. Repeat steps 6 and 7 for each field that you want to include in your new table. In our example, we've added: CommonName, Genus, Species, Flowering, LightPreference, FertilizeFrequency, WateringFrequency, DatePurchased, PlacePurchased, DatePlanted, and Notes.

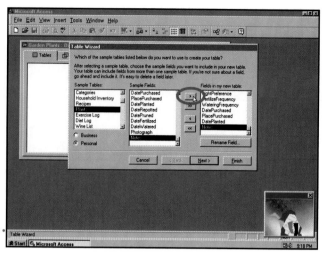

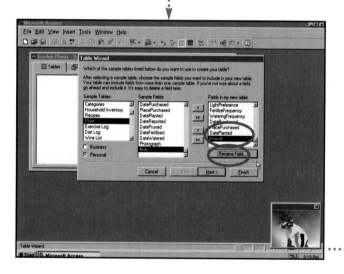

8 To rename a field, select the **Notes** field name in the Fields in my new table list box and click the **Rename Field** button. In the Rename Field dialog box, type the name **Remarks** in the text box and click the **OK** button. Access inserts the new field name into the Fields in my new table list box. After you have entered all the fileds you want in the new table, click the **Next >** button.

9 The Table Wizard chooses a default name for your table and prompts you to set a primary key for the table. To change the default name, simply type a new name into the text box. We've used the name Plants for this table. Allow the Table Wizard to set the primary key by clicking the **Yes, set a primary key for me** option. Click the **Next >** button to move on to the next dialog box.

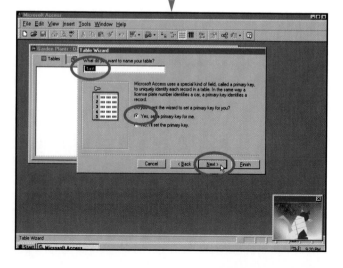

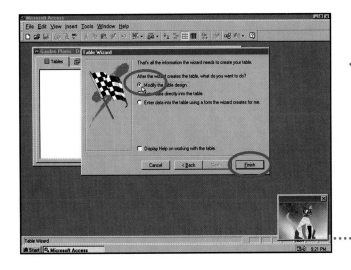

10 The final Table Wizard dialog box appears. Select the **Modify the table design** option button so that the table will be opened in the Design View window, enabling you to make additional modifications to the table's definition (see Task 13). Click the **Finish** button.

11 Access completes your table and opens it in the Design view window. This is the same window that you would use to create a table without the help of the Table Wizard. ■

Puzzled?

You can easily modify a table at any time. Select the table from the Database window and click the Design button.

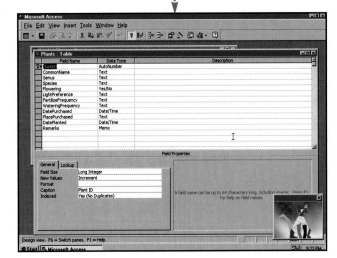

Missing Link

In the last table wizard screen, select **the Enter data directly into the table** option button if you want to immediately begin to enter data into the table. The **Enter data into the table using a form the wizard creates for me** option causes the wizard to build a simple form that you can use to enter data into the table. If you want the Office Assistant to help you enter data into the table click the checkbox at the bottom of the dialog box.

TASK 13

Adding a New Field in Design View

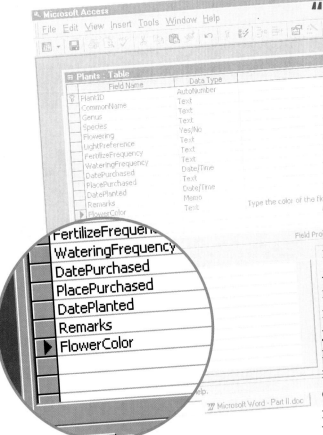

"Why would I do this?"

When using the various Wizards, there will often be times that you will have to make additional changes manually. In our Plants table example, the Table Wizard's pre-defined table does not have a field for all of the information that we want to store about plants, such as the flower's color.

To add a new field to a table, you must use the Design view option and add the field yourself. When you add fields, Access requires that you provide the field a name, and some additional formatting information. Use a name for your field that is descriptive of the information which you plan to store in it. Field names can be a maximum of 64 characters in length. Just like other names, you can use any combination of letters, numbers, spaces and other characters. The only characters which are excluded from your use are: leading spaces in the name, periods (.), exclamation points (!), brackets ([ ]), or grave accents (`).

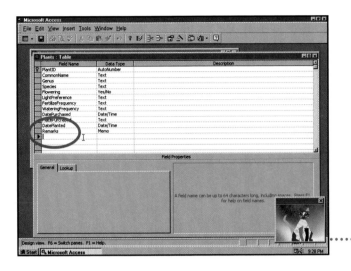

1 Click the mouse pointer in the first empty row in the Field Name column. This should be just below the field named Remarks. This is where you will enter your new field name.

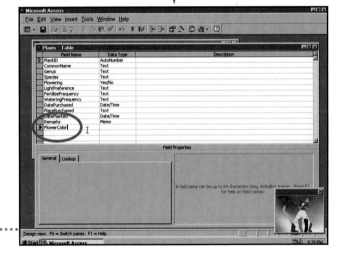

2 Type **FlowerColor** in the empty space.

3 Press the **Tab** key to move to the Data Type column. Click the arrow button which is now displayed. This will show you a drop-down list of available data type options. Select the **Text** option for your new field. This is also the default data type option.

Task 13: Adding a New Field in Design View

4 Press the **Tab** key again to move to the Description column. Type **Type the color of the flower when in full bloom here.** This is the descriptive text for the FlowerColor field.

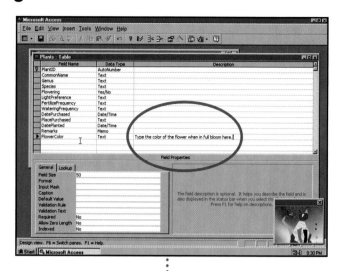

Puzzled?

Access will display these descriptions in the status bar when the person using your database enters information in this field. You can always change a description if you find that it doesn't meet your needs.

5 Press **F6** to switch from the upper to the lower pane of this window. You now see the cursor in the Field Size property text box. The Field Size property enables you to specify the length of the field in number of characters. Enter **20** for the size. ■

Missing Link

The maximum length for a text field is 255 characters; the default length is 50. Don't arbitrarily set a text field to 255 characters. If you set a very large number for the field size, Access uses that number to allocate memory and disk storage. The fewer characters you set for the field size, the less memory and disk space the field will take up.

Working with Numbers

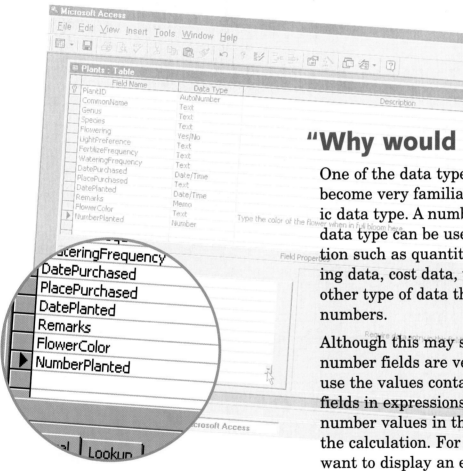

"Why would I do this?"

One of the data types that you will become very familiar with is the numeric data type. A number or a numeric data type can be used to store information such as quantities of products, pricing data, cost data, temperature, or any other type of data that is expressed in numbers.

Although this may seem to be limiting, number fields are very useful. You can use the values contained in number fields in expressions that use the stored number values in these fields for part of the calculation. For example, you may want to display an extended price on an invoice. This can be done by using anexpression that multiplies the value contained in the quantity field by the value contained in the price field. Calculated values such as an extended price should never be stored as a value in a table. Date/Time and Currency data types are subtypes of numeric fields.

Working with Numbers

1 Move the cursor to the next blank row in the Field Name column by clicking the row with the mouse pointer. Type **NumberPlanted** and press the **Tab** key.

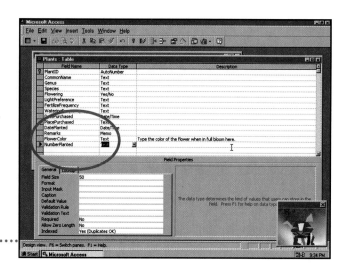

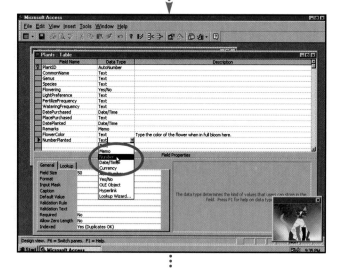

2 Click the arrow button in the Data Type column to display the drop-down list. Select **Number** as the data type for this field.

Puzzled?

The Byte option for Field Size enables you to enter any positive, whole number between 0 and 255. For help using the Field Size property, press the F1 Key.

3 Press **F6**, or click the Field Size text box, and click the arrow button to display the drop-down list box. Select the **Byte** option.

Missing Link

For number fields, the Field Size property enables you to choose the type of number. The range of numbers which you can enter in this field is determined by the choice you make for the Field Size.

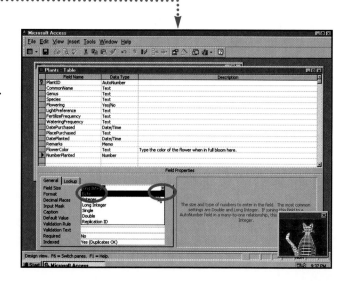

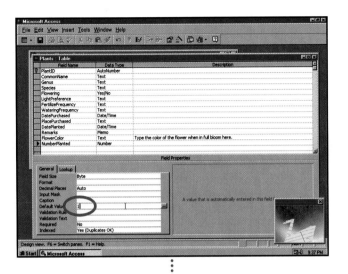

Puzzled?

For a field which will contain only dates and/or times, select the **Data/Time** data type. A date field holds any date from January 1, 100 to December 31, 9999.

4 Click the **Default Value** text box and type the number **1**. This value will be automatically entered by Access into this field when you create a new record. You can always override a default value by typing in a different value.

Missing Link

The default value of 1 is used because we are assuming that you buy at least one of each plant. If you simply are entering information into your table for possible use later, you can override the default value and enter a 0.

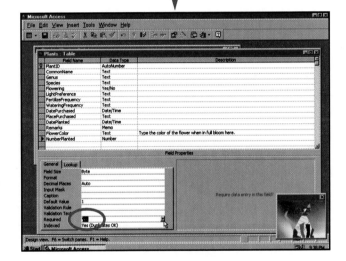

5 Move down to the **Required** text box, and click the arrow button. Choose **Yes**. This property setting requires that you enter a value into the field before you can update and save a record. This will ensure that if you override the default value, you are required to enter another in the field—even if it is a zero. ■

Missing Link

Remember, you can go back and change a value in a table if you enter an incorrect number, or if you forget to enter a number different than the default value.

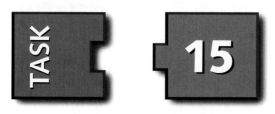

Using a Yes/No Field

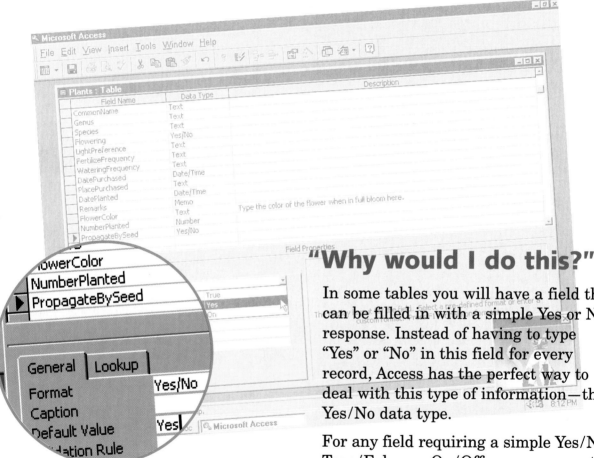

"Why would I do this?"

In some tables you will have a field that can be filled in with a simple Yes or No response. Instead of having to type "Yes" or "No" in this field for every record, Access has the perfect way to deal with this type of information—the Yes/No data type.

For any field requiring a simple Yes/No, True/False, or On/Off response, use the Yes/No data type. This data type can be represented in the table or on a form as a text box, which requires you to type in the response "Yes" or "No". You can also represent this data type as a check box, where a check mark indicates a "Yes" response, or as a combo box, where you can select the correct response from a drop-down menu.

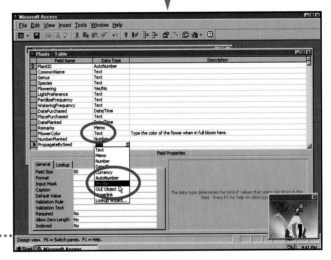

1 Move down to the next blank field row in the Field Name column. Type the field name **PropagateBySeed**.

Missing Link

By using a Yes/No type of field, you can help to eliminate data entry errors by allowing users to select only one of two responses.

2 Move to the Data Type column and click the arrow button and select **Yes/No** from the drop-down list.

Puzzled?

If you know the name of the data type that you want to select, you can also type in the first letter or two, and Access will fill in the rest for you. For example, if you type the letter Y, Access fills in Yes/No.

3 In the Field Properties pane, select the **Format** text box, click the arrow button, and choose the **Yes/No** option. In our example, this is the most appropriate answer for the user to give for this particular field.

Puzzled?

You can access a drop-down list from your keyboard by pressing the **Alt+down-arrow key** combination. Then use the up and down arrow keys to select a specific option.

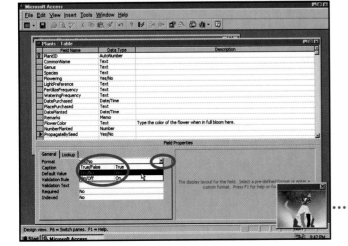

61

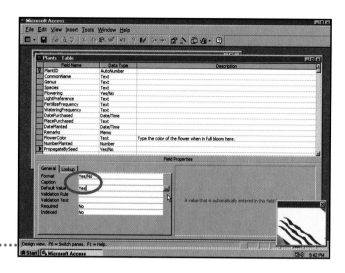

4 Move down to the Default Value text box and type **Yes**.

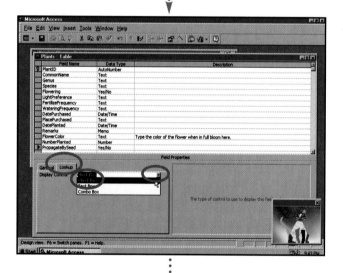

5 Click the **Lookup** tab to view a new group of property options. The Yes/No data type has only one, Display Control. Click the arrow button and select **Checkbox** from the list. This is also the default option. This field will now be displayed as a check box in both the table and form views. Checking the box is the same as typing "Yes," while removing the check mark it is the same as typing "No."

6 Click on the field **Flowering** and then on its property **Lookup** tab. Type **Yes** in the Default Value property box. Select **Checkbox** for this yes/no field. ■

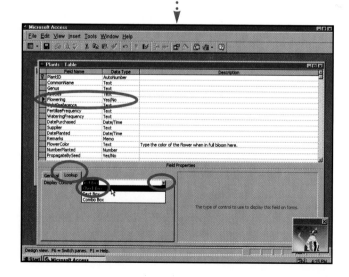

Saving the New Table Definition

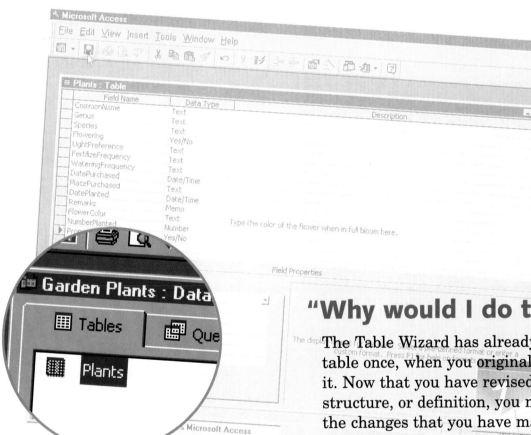

"Why would I do this?"

The Table Wizard has already saved the table once, when you originally created it. Now that you have revised the table's structure, or definition, you must save the changes that you have made before exiting from the Access application.

When you save a table, Access writes the table's definition to your hard disk. The names of the fields, and their various properties which you have assigned make up a table's definition. Once you save the table, Access builds the table, making it ready for your use.

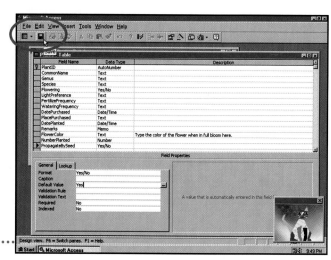

1 Click the **Save** button on the toolbar. If you closely watch the status bar at the bottom of the window, you will see messages displayed as Access completes each procedure necessary for saving your table.

2 You can also save a table's definition by choosing **Save** from the **File** menu, or by using the keyboard combination **Ctrl+S**.

Missing Link

If you are not finished with your changes to the table definition, you can continue to add new fields or change properties and simply save the revised definition again.

3 When you have finished making any changes to your table, click the **Close** button (**X**) at the upper right corner of the Design view window (not the Access application). You will now see the new table, Plants, in the Tables list. ■

Puzzled?

If you create a table from scratch, you will see a dialog box asking you to enter a name for the table. Since you created this table with the help of the Table Wizard, it already has a name. You'll learn to create a table from scratch in Task 23.

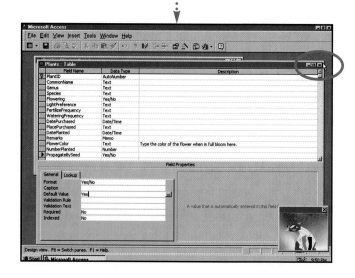

Opening a Table

"Why would I do this?"

Once you have created a table, you must open it in order to work with it—just like you open the Access application to use the databases and tables it contains. An unopened table is similar to an unopened ledger or order pad; you can't work with either one until you open it.

1 Click the **Tables** tab on the Database window so that the Tables list is visible to you. Select a table by clicking it—either on the icon or the label.

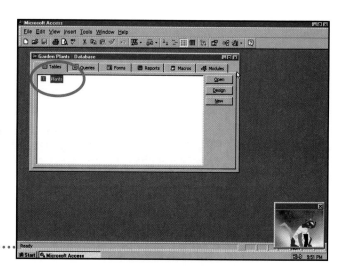

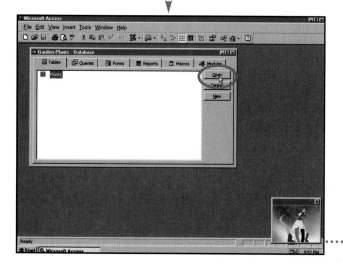

2 Click the **Open** button on the Database window.

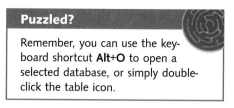

Puzzled?

Remember, you can use the keyboard shortcut **Alt+O** to open a selected database, or simply double-click the table icon.

3 The Plants table appears in datasheet view. ■

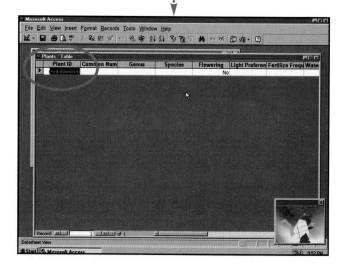

Changing a Field Name

"Why would I do this?"

As you begin to work with a table, you may find that one or more of the field labels at the top of the table is not quite as descriptive as you might want it to be. Or even worse, you may find that you accidentally misspelled a field label.

If a field does not immediately describe what type of data is supposed to be placed in it, you might want to change the field's column label.

Task 18: Changing a Field Name

1 Be sure that you select the **Tables** tab on the Database window. Double-click the **Plants** table icon to open it in Datasheet view.

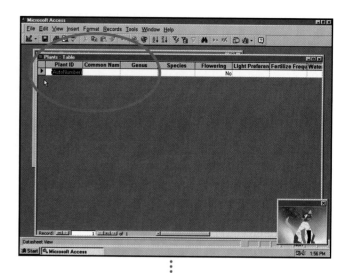

> **Puzzled?**
>
> Remember, you can also open a table by selecting it and clicking the **Open** button on the Database window, or by pressing the keyboard combination **Alt+O**.

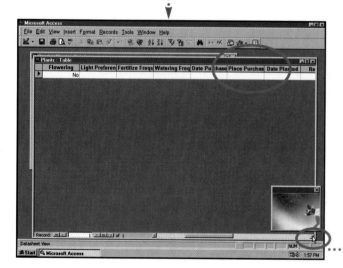

2 Click the right scroll bar button at the bottom of the table window until you see the field column label **Place Purchased** displayed on the top of the table.

> **Puzzled?**
>
> If you scroll too far, simply click the left scroll bar button to bring the field back in view. It doesn't matter if the field is in the middle of the window or on one side or the other.

3 Move the mouse pointer to the Place Purchased column label and click the right mouse button. A shortcut menu is displayed.

> **Missing Link**
>
> Right-clicking the mouse will, in most cases, display a shortcut menu. The options available to you on this menu will vary depending on what you are currently doing, or on the object that is currently selected.

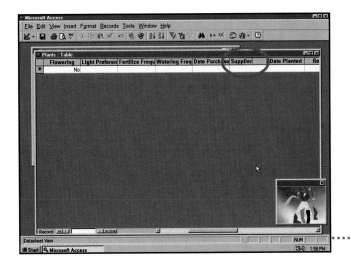

4 Click the **Rename Column** option from the shortcut menu. This will place the column label in edit mode; a blinking cursor is displayed at the beginning of the field name. Type **Supplier** as the new field label.

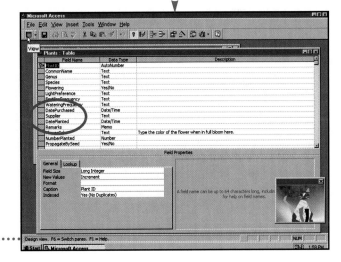

5 Click the View button on the toolbar to see the changed label in Design View.

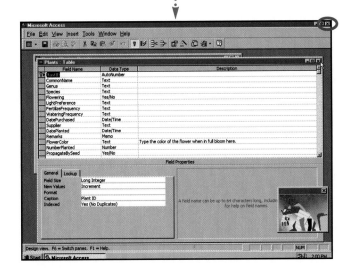

6 To close the table, click the **Close** button (**X**). The field name revision you made is automatically saved by Access. ∎

19

Moving a Field Within a Table

"Why would I do this?"

There will be times after you have worked with a table for a short time, that you will find that the fields are not in the right order for natural data entry. For example, you may input data from a handwritten form that includes a client's Social Security number, last name, and first name. Unfortunately, your table's fields are in a first name, last name, and Social Security number order.

The discrepancy between the written form and table requires some fancy eyeball gymnastics that can get very tiring by day's end. You can easily adjust the order of the fields in a table in just a few simple steps.

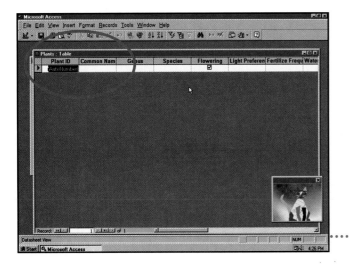

1 Open the **Plants** table by selecting the table in the Database window. Click the **Open** button. The table will open in the normal Datasheet view.

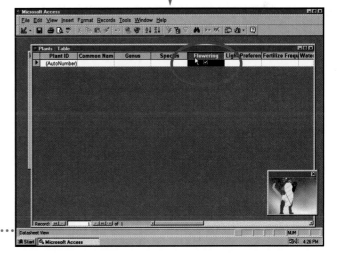

2 Select the column header **Flowering** by clicking it once. Notice that Access highlights the entire column.

3 Drag the field to the left of the Genus field. You will see a thick vertical bar showing the field's new location between the Common Name and Genus columns.

Puzzled?

To drag an object, select it by pressing and holding the left mouse button as you move the mouse to the object's new location. Here you see a stylized object moving along with the mouse pointer.

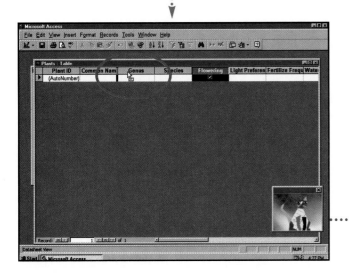

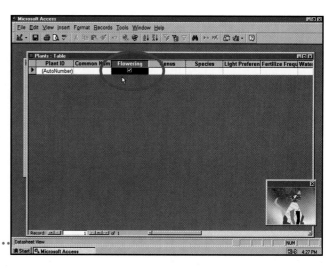

4 Set the field into its new location by releasing the mouse button. You can save the table's new format by clicking the Save button at this time. But don't do this yet.

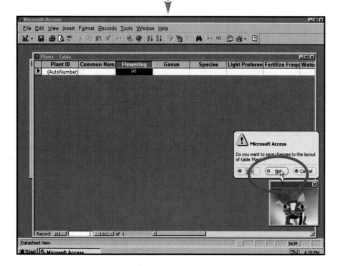

5 In our example, we do not want to save the new column order. Click the **Close** button (**X**). The Office Assistant displays a balloon asking you if you want to save the new format. Click the **No** button. The columns in the table revert back to their original order and the table is closed. ■

Missing Link

You can change the order of the columns in any table at any time. Changing the column order does not affect any of the information contained in the table, nor does it affect any other object that is based on the table.

Inserting a Field

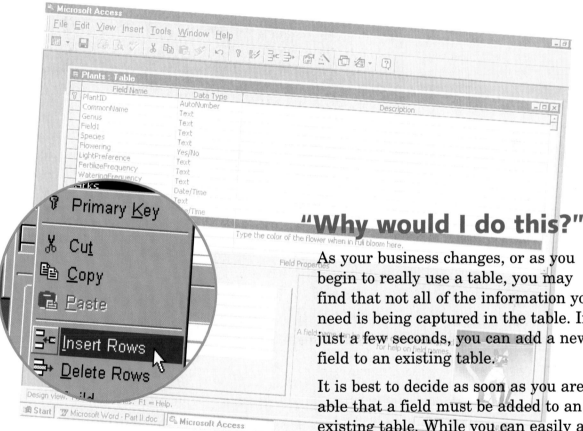

"Why would I do this?"

As your business changes, or as you begin to really use a table, you may find that not all of the information you need is being captured in the table. In just a few seconds, you can add a new field to an existing table.

It is best to decide as soon as you are able that a field must be added to an existing table. While you can easily add a new field to any table, it can take a great deal of time to add this information to the previously existing records if you have already entered several hundred records into the table. While there are ways that it can be accomplished, it is better to decide on a table's ultimate format as early as possible so that you don't have to go back and add the new information to many records.

Task 20: Inserting a Field

1 Select the **Plants** table and then click the mouse on the **Design** button on the Database window. The table will be opened in the Design view mode. Click the selector button for the **Remarks** field. The entire row is selected.

> **Missing Link**
>
> To insert a new field between two existing fields, move the row selector (the arrow beside the field name) to the field which will become the field *below* your newly inserted field.

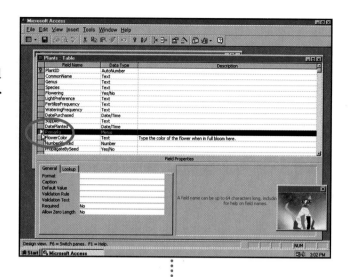

2 With the mouse pointer still located on the selector button for the Remarks field, click the right mouse button, displaying a short-cut menu.

> **Puzzled?**
>
> You can also make many of the same selections from the toolbar or menu that you can make from the shortcut menu. It is often easier to use the shortcut menu because you do not have to move the mouse from its current location up to the menu or toolbar.

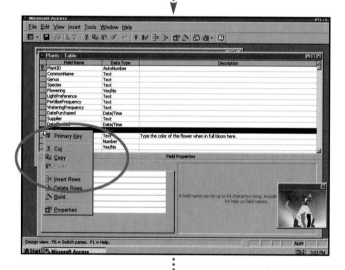

3 Select the **Insert Rows** option from the shortcut menu. Access will insert a new row immediately above the currently selected row. All of the rows below the newly inserted blank row move down.

> **Missing Link**
>
> Multiple rows can be inserted by dragging down as many selector buttons as you want rows. For example, if you wanted to insert two rows, then you would have selected the Remarks selector button, dragging down to FlowerColor's button, highlighting two rows. Access would then insert two new rows.

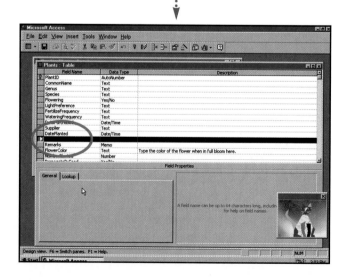

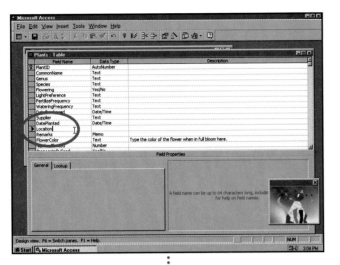

4 Click the mouse pointer in the **Field Name** column of the new row. Type **Location** as the name for the new field.

5 Press the **Tab** key and choose **Text** for the Data Type for the new field. (If you want to make any changes to the field's properties in the lower pane of this window, press **F6**.)

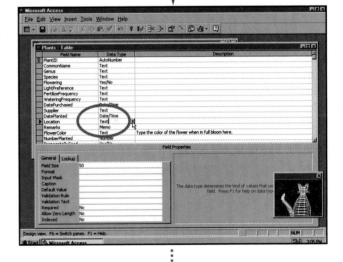

Missing Link

If you decide that you do not want to use this field, select the **No** button when Access prompts you to save your changes to this table, or simply delete this field with the **Delete Rows** button on the toolbar or the **Delete Rows** option on the shortcut menu.

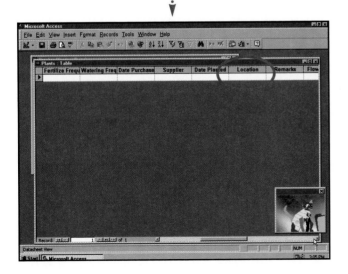

6 Click the **Save** button to save the table's revised definition. Now click the **View** button again to return to Datasheet view. By scrolling toward the right edge of the table you will see your new field listed. ■

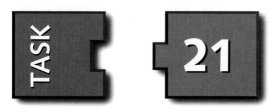

Adding a New Field in Datasheet View

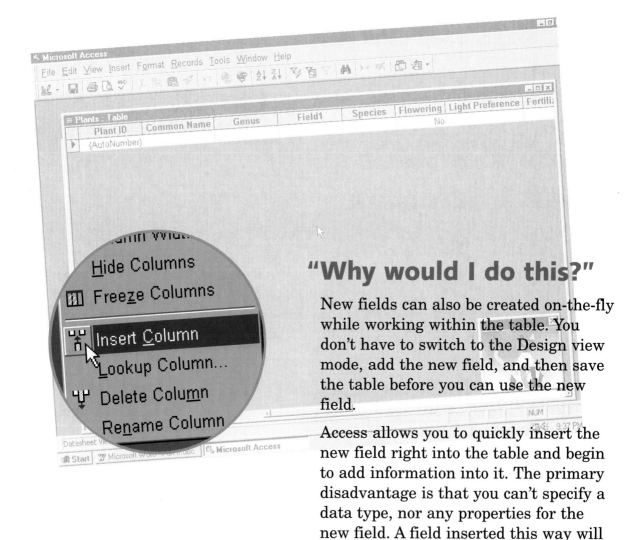

"Why would I do this?"

New fields can also be created on-the-fly while working within the table. You don't have to switch to the Design view mode, add the new field, and then save the table before you can use the new field.

Access allows you to quickly insert the new field right into the table and begin to add information into it. The primary disadvantage is that you can't specify a data type, nor any properties for the new field. A field inserted this way will automatically be a text data type. However, this doesn't prevent you from entering number data and later changing the data type to number.

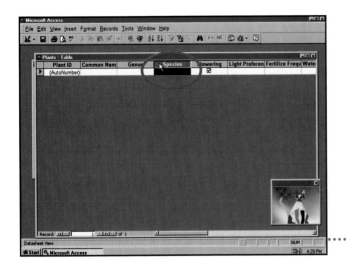

1 Open the **Plants** table in Datasheet view if it is not already open. Move the mouse pointer to the field label **Species** and click it once, selecting the column.

2 Right-click the mouse on the column label to display the shortcut menu. Choose the **Insert Column** option. You will see Access insert a column with a very generic label of **Field 1**.

Missing Link

You have already learned to rename a column by selecting it and then selecting the Rename Column option from the shortcut menu (see Task 18).

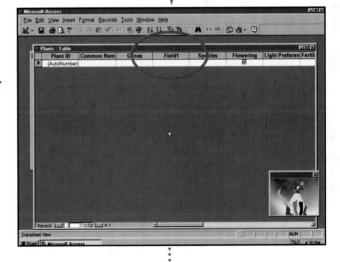

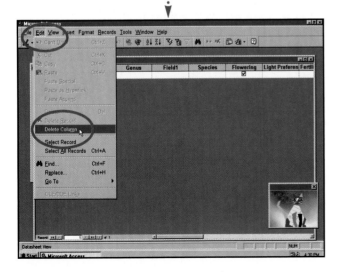

3 At this time we don't need a column labeled Field 1, so select **Edit** from the menu bar, and then choose **Delete Column** from the drop-down menu. Click the **Yes** button in the balloon when the Office Assistant asks you if you want to permanently delete this column. ■

77

Deleting a Field

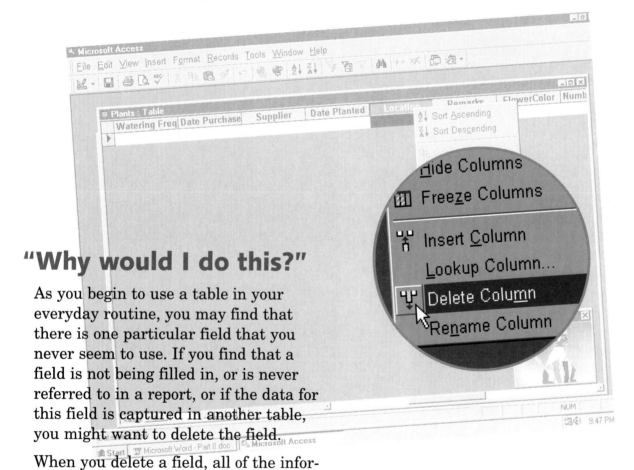

"Why would I do this?"

As you begin to use a table in your everyday routine, you may find that there is one particular field that you never seem to use. If you find that a field is not being filled in, or is never referred to in a report, or if the data for this field is captured in another table, you might want to delete the field.

When you delete a field, all of the information contained in it will be lost from all records contained in the table. Any references to the field made by other tables, or Access objects, will generate errors. You will have to track any errors down and correct the fields so that they refer to another field in the current table or a different one.

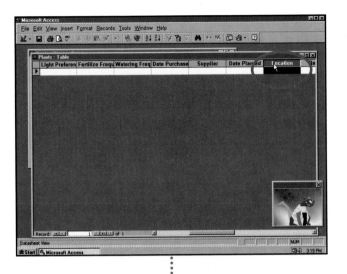

1 Open the **Plants** table in the Datasheet view. Scroll through the table until you find the field **Location**. Select the field by clicking its column label.

Puzzled?

After you save the revised table definition, you will not be able to recover any of the field's information, so be very sure that you have selected the right field for deletion.

2 Click the right mouse button, displaying the shortcut menu again. Select **Delete Column** from the menu. Access will immediately delete the column from the table definition. ■

Missing Link

Be absolutely sure that you want to delete this column and any data contained in it. You can always make a copy of the entire table using the Copy and Paste commands—simply give the copy a new name when prompted.

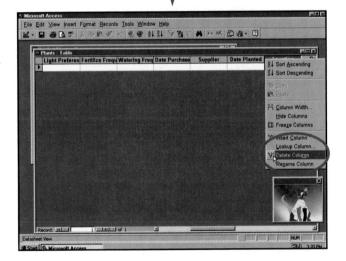

TASK 23

Building a Table from Scratch

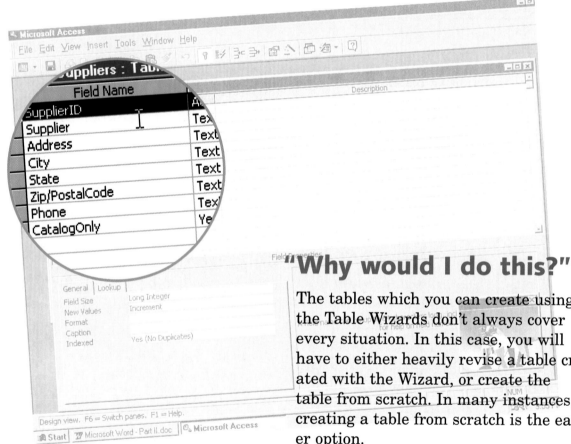

"Why would I do this?"

The tables which you can create using the Table Wizards don't always cover every situation. In this case, you will have to either heavily revise a table created with the Wizard, or create the table from scratch. In many instances, creating a table from scratch is the easier option.

By designing a table completely in Design view, you can quickly create a unique table that does not require extensive revisions or additions. You have complete control over all of the properties for each field, enabling you to customize a table to the greatest degree.

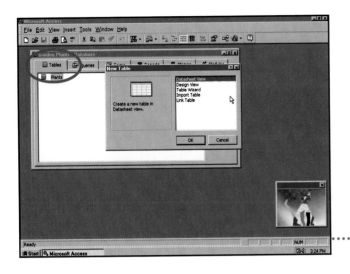

1 Be sure that the **Tables** tab is selected on the Database window. Click the **New** button, displaying the New Table dialog box.

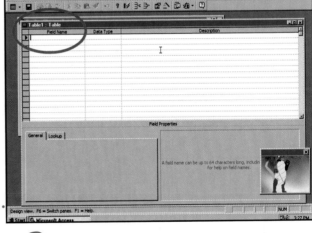

2 Choose the **Design View** option from the list and click the **OK** button. This will open the Design view window for creating a new table.

3 Type **SupplierID** as the Field Name in the first row. This will be the identifying, or *primary key*, field for this table. Press the **Tab** key and choose **AutoNumber** as the data type.

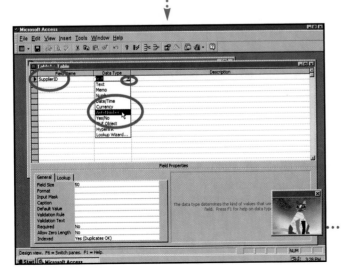

Missing Link

The AutoNumber data type is often used to provide a unique, identifying value for every record in a table. One of the secrets of a successful database is to ensure that each record in a table is unique.

81

4 Add the following fields in this order: **Supplier**, **Address**, **City**, **State**, **Zip/PostalCode**, and **Phone**. Each field will use the default data type—Text.

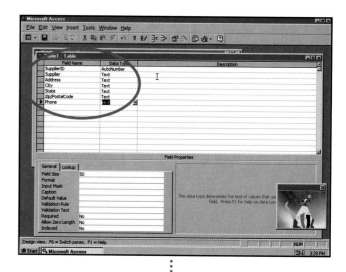

Puzzled?

If you notice a typo in one of your field names, simply select the field name and retype it. Editing the field name does not affect any of the field properties or data types you have already set.

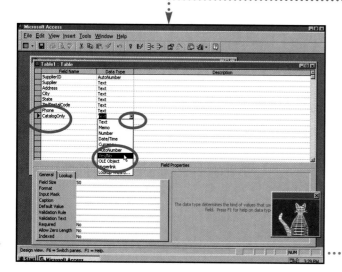

5 Type **CatalogOnly** in the Field Name column as the last field. Select the data type **Yes/No**.

6 Click the selector button for the first field, **SupplierID**, to select it. This selects the entire row and shows you that you have selected the correct field.

Puzzled?

If you miss with the mouse and select the wrong row, just move the mouse and click again. The previous row will become unselected, and the new row will be selected.

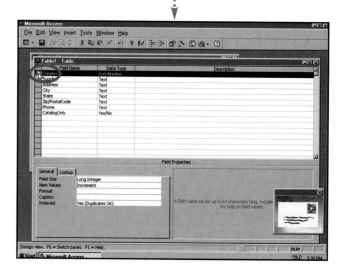

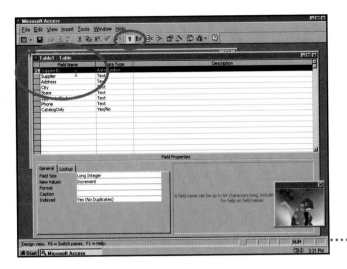

7 Right click the mouse, displaying a short-cut menu. Select the **Primary Key** option. You will see a small key symbol displayed on the SupplierID selector button's face. By setting this field as the primary key, you can link it to the foreign key in another table.

8 Now that the table has been completed, click the **Save** button on the toolbar. The Save As dialog box is now displayed. Type **Plant Suppliers** into the text box, over-writing the default table name of **Table1**.

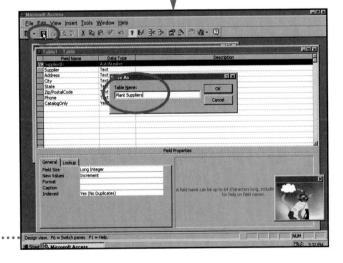

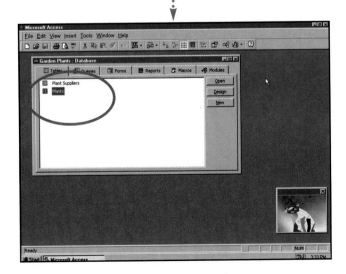

9 Click the **OK** button to save the new table's definition, and then close the table by clicking the window's **Close** button (**X**). You will be able to now see the new table listed in the Database window. ■

PART III

Entering and Editing Data

24 Entering New Information in a Table

25 Copying Information from Another Record

26 Editing Data in a Field

27 Undoing an Edit

28 Searching for Information

29 Replacing Selected Information

30 Sorting Records

31 Using Filters

32 Filtering by Form

33 Deleting a Selected Record

34 Resizing Rows and Columns

35 Freezing and Unfreezing Columns

36 Hiding and Unhiding Columns

▲ ● ■ ● ▲ ● ● ■ ▲ ●

N THE PREVIOUS TWO PARTS OF THIS BOOK, you have created a database and placed two tables in it. These tables can now be populated with data. When you add information into a table, you normally will enter all of the data necessary for a single record, and then move on to the next one. Remember, each row of the table is a separate record. You can think of each record as a single, blank sheet of paper. Once you fill in the information necessary for the record, you can turn to the next blank page and enter the next record.

Each distinct piece of information in the record is recorded in its own field. Each field fills a single block of the paper form. As you complete the information for a field, you move on to the next block. For example, in the Plants table in Part II, you have fields for Common Name, Genus, Species, and other information related to each plant. The second table, Plant Suppliers, stores information about each supplier, name, address, and other pertinent information that relates to each of the individual businesses from which you buy your plants. The AutoNumber field uniquely numbers each individual record; in the Plants table, it is the Plant ID field, and, in the Plant Suppliers table, it is SupplierID.

With a database file you can easily add new information to fields and records, and change the information with just a few keystrokes. You can change the appearance of your information by using a different font, or by modifying the height of your rows, or the width of your columns. If necessary, you can hide selected fields of information from view. This is especially helpful if you work with information of a sensitive nature. For example, suppose you work with personnel or payroll records and want to show a colleague some aspect of the information, but not specific personal data. With Access you can hide the personal data from view.

The most common way to enter information in your Access table is by typing it in with your keyboard. After you become more familiar with Access, you may want to enter information by importing data from other programs. You can even add pictures to your records. This can be very handy if you are creating a database table for products that you sell.

In addition to being able to store large amounts of data in a table, one of the most important functions of a database, is its capability to find and then easily update the information when some part of the record changes. With Access, you can use the powerful Find command to search for a specific record or groups of records.

Also, unlike your pad of paper records, each on their own page, you can easily sort all of your records by any field that you choose. In the case of the Plants table, you can quickly sort your list of plants by their common name, by genus, the date they were planted, by their flower color, or any other field that you select. You can sort the records in either an ascending or a descending order. An ascending sort order is similar to the normal alphabetical order that you are used to, except that numbers come before letters. A descending sort order is the reverse of ascending: letters beginning with Z come first and numbers, ending with the smallest negative number.

In Task 24, "Entering New Information in a Table," you will need to enter the information contained in the following tables. These tables include the information for the records that you will use throughout most of the tasks in this book. Be sure to enter this information exactly as shown, including any mistakes or typos.

Common Name	Genus	Species	Flowering	Light Preference	Fertilize Frequency	Watering Frequency
Amethyst Flower	Browallia	speciosa	Yes ☑	Shade, Filtered Sun	Weekly	Weekly
Butterfly Bbush	buddleia	alternifolia	Yes ☑	Full Sun	Annually	Keep Dry
Canterbury Bell	Campanula	medium	Yes ☑	Full Sun, Filtered Sun	Monthly	Weekly
Costmary	Chrysanthemum	balsamita	Yes ☑	Full Sun	Monthly	Weekly
Foxglove	Digitalis	purpurea	Yes ☑	Shade, Filtered Sun	Annually	Weekly
Purple Coneflower	Echinacea	purpurea	Yes ☑	Full Sun	Monthly	Weekly
Cranesbill	Geranium	himalayense	Yes ☑	Full Sun	Monthly	Weekly
Lotus	Nelumbo	nucifera	Yes ☑	Full Sun, Filtered Sun	Annually	Keep Wet
catnip	Nepeta	cataria	Yes ☑	Full Sun	Monthly	Weekly
Wormwood	Artemisia	absinthium	Yes ☑	Full Sun	Monthly	Keep Dry

Common Name	Date Purchased	Place Purchased	Date Planted	Remarks	Flower Color	Number Planted	Propagate by Seed
Amethyst Flower	3/1/96	Portland Plants	3/2/96	Annual, may be perennial	Blue	6	Yes ☑
Butterfly Bush	5/15/93	Portland Plants	5/20/93	Perennial	Blue	2	No
Canterbury Bell	12/10/94	Nichol's Plants & Seeds	2/1/95	Biennial	Blue, Pink, White	15	Yes ☑
Costmary	3/15/95	NW Hardy Plants	3/15/95	Perennial		3	No
Foxglove	5/1/93	N/A	6/1/93	Biennial, Perennial	Purple	12	Yes ☑
Purple Coneflower	3/1/95	Portland Plants	3/2/95	Perennial	Purple	3	Yes ☑
Cranesbill	6/1/94	St. John's Perennials	6/1/94	Perennial	Lilac	2	No
Lotus	3/15/95	Portland Pond's	3/15/95	Perennial	Pink	2	Yes
catnip	6/1/93	St. John's Perennials	6/1/93	Perennial	White	6	Yes ☑
Wormwood	4/1/94	St. John's Perennials	4/1/94	Perennial	Yellow	1	Yes ☑

Entering New Information in a Table

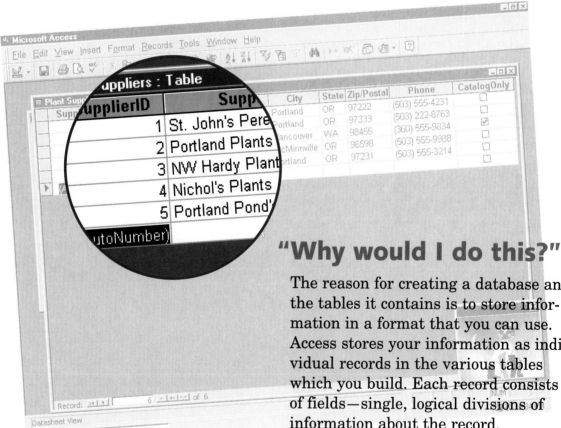

"Why would I do this?"

The reason for creating a database and the tables it contains is to store information in a format that you can use. Access stores your information as individual records in the various tables which you build. Each record consists of fields—single, logical divisions of information about the record.

When you fill out a paper form, you are completing a record. Each block that you complete is a specific field, whether it be a name, address, date or quantity. Information is entered into the table by typing it into each of the fields, and records.

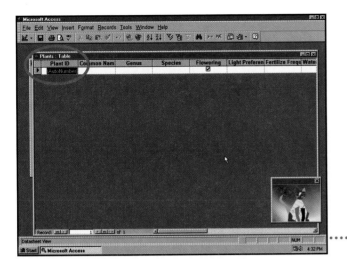

1 Start Access, open the **Garden Plants** database, and then open the **Plants** table. You must always open a table before you can begin to enter or edit information in it.

2 Because there are no records in this table, only one record row is displayed. Press the **Tab** key to move the cursor from the Plant ID field to the Common Name field. Remember, the Plant ID field uses the AutoNumber data type and so doesn't require, nor allow, any input. (Notice the (AutoNumber) displayed in the field.) Access will fill this field automatically when you enter information in the first field.

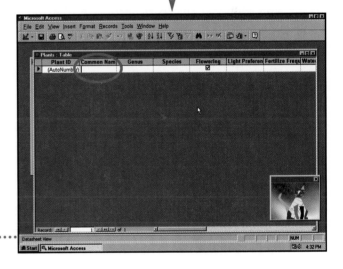

3 Type **Sweet William** in the Common Name field. Press **Tab** to move the cursor. You have entered data into a field, so Access assigns a number to the Plant ID field.

Puzzled?

A record doesn't have to have every field completed. You can fill in missing information later.

4 Type the following pressing the **Tab** key after each entry: Genus: **Diantus**; Species: **barbatus**; Flowering: ☑; Light Preference: **Full Sun**; Fertilize Frequency: **Monthly**; Watering Frequency: **Keep Moist**; Date Purchased: **3/5/96**; Supplier: **St. John's Perennials**; Date Planted: **3/11/96**; Remarks: **Perennial**; FlowerColor: **Pink**; NumberPlanted: **6**; PropagateBySeed: ☑.

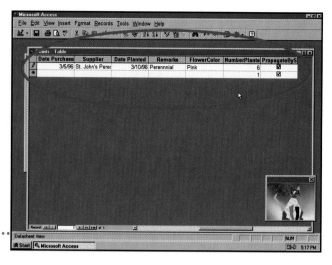

5 Press the **Tab** key one more time to complete the record. When you leave the last field of the record, Access automatically saves it. Complete the information for the table by using the data contained in the tables at the beginning of this part. Follow steps 1 through 5 for each record.

> **Missing Link**
>
> A checkbox can also be filled with a Yes by pressing the Spacebar on your keyboard.

6 Close the Plants table by clicking the **Close (X)** button.

> **Missing Link**
>
> If you make a mistake when entering information into a field, simply press **Shift+Tab** to move back to the field and retype the data.

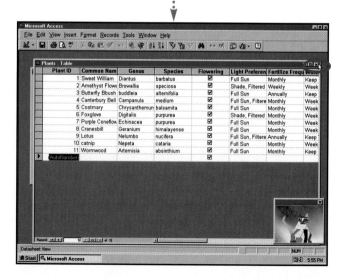

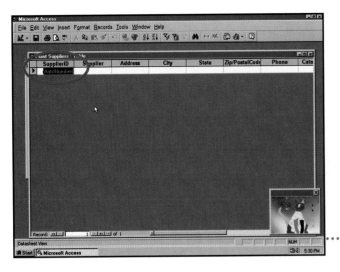

7 Open the Suppliers table by double-clicking its icon in the Database window. This will open the Suppliers table in the Datasheet view.

8 Press the **Tab** key to move from the SupplierID field to the Supplier Name field and enter the information shown in the table below. Use the techniques you have already learned in this task. ■

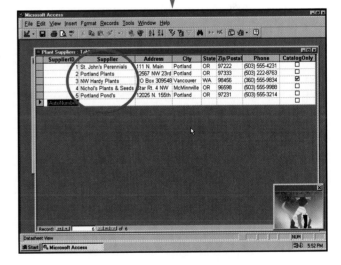

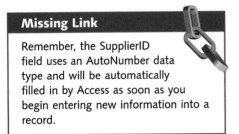

Missing Link

Remember, the SupplierID field uses an AutoNumber data type and will be automatically filled in by Access as soon as you begin entering new information into a record.

Supplier	Address	City	State	Zip/Postal Code	Phone	Catalog Only
St. John's Perennials	111 N. Main	Portland	OR	97222	(503) 555-4231	(empty)
Portland Plants	42567 NW 23rd	Portland	OR	97333	(503) 222-8763	(empty)
NW Hardy Plants	PO Box 309548	Vancouver	WA	98456	(360) 555-9834	☑
Nichol's Plants & Seeds	Star Rt. 4 NW	McMinnville	OR	96598	(503) 555-9988	(empty)

Copying Information from Another Record

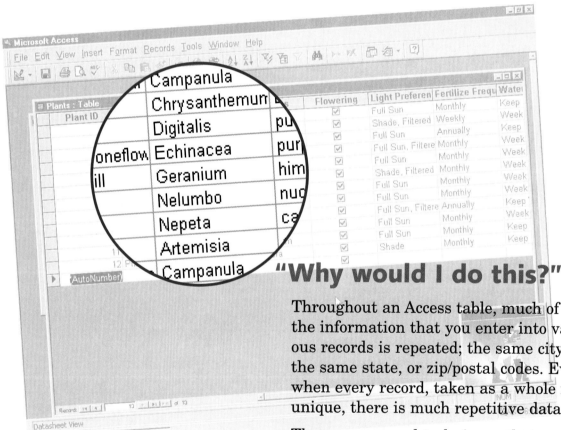

"Why would I do this?"

Throughout an Access table, much of the information that you enter into various records is repeated; the same city, the same state, or zip/postal codes. Even when every record, taken as a whole is unique, there is much repetitive data.

There are several techniques that you can use while entering or editing information which allow you to copy information from one record to another, without having to retype it each time. This will save you much valuable time, and help alleviate any errors from miskeying information.

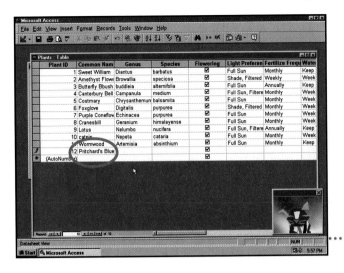

1 Open the Plants table if not already open. Place the mouse pointer in the blank field at the bottom of the **Common Name** column, and click once. Type **Pritchard's Blue** and press the **Tab** key to move to the next field.

2 Now move the mouse pointer up to the **Genus** field for plant number 4, Canterbury Bell, and click once. You will see the blinking insertion point in this cell. The insertion point's actual location within the cell depends upon where you place the mouse pointer when you click. Press the **Home** key to move the insertion point to the beginning of the word Campanula.

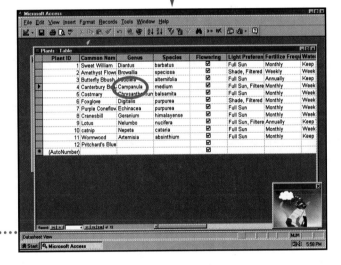

3 Press and hold the **Shift** key, and press the **End** key. This will select the entire entry in this cell. Let both keys go. Remember, when a cell and its contents appear on a black background with white text, it means the cell and its contents have been selected.

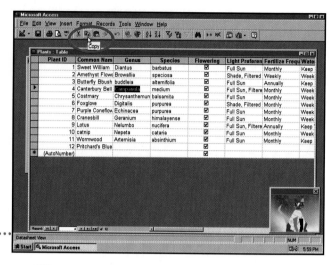

4 Click the **Copy** button on the toolbar. This copies the text in the selected cell to the Windows Clipboard, where it will remain until you either replace it with another selection or you exit from Windows 95.

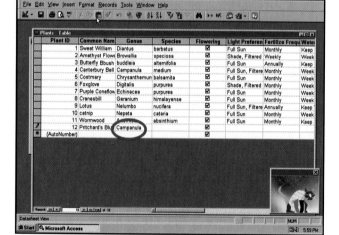

5 Move the mouse pointer down to the **Genus** field for the new record at plant number 12 and click. Click the **Paste** button on the toolbar. Access will immediately copy the contents of the Windows Clipboard to the selected cell.

Puzzled?

If you want to simply copy the contents of the cell directly above the current cell, simply use the keyboard combination **Ctrl+'** (Ctrl key plus either a single or double quote key). Access copies and inserts the data from the cell directly above the current cell.

6 Type the remaining information: Species: **lactiflora**; Flowering: ☑; Light Preference: **Shade**; Fertilize Frequency: **Monthly**; Watering Frequency: **Keep moist**; Date Purchased: **4/1/95**; Supplier: **St. John's Perennials**; Date Planted: **4/1/95**; Remarks: **Perennial**; FlowerColor: **Blue**; NumberPlanted: **3**; and PropagateBySeed: ☑. ■

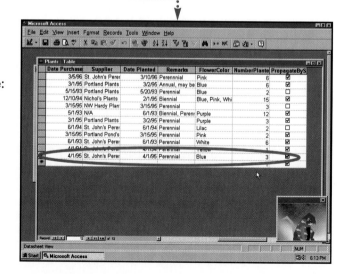

Editing Data in a Field

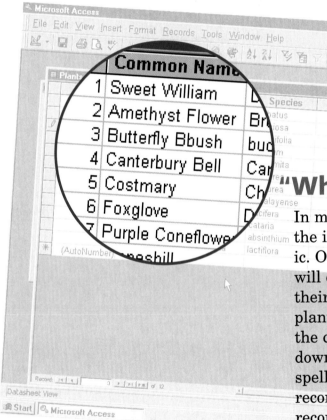

"Why would I do this?"

In most databases that you will create, the information they contain is not static. Over time, some of the information will change; companies move or change their phone numbers, the number of plants you have increases or decreases, the cost of an item you sell goes up or down. You may find that you have misspelled some piece of data in one of your records, or you may want to complete a record in which you did not have information to fill in a field(s).

Any of these will give you cause to edit, or update, a record in a table. Editing information can include correcting an erroneous entry, adding new information, deleting a record, or any other change necessary to keep the data contained in a table accurate.

1 Click the mouse pointer in the Common Name field for plant number 3. The entry now reads Butterfly Bbush. Needless to say, the word "bush" isn't supposed to have two "b"s in it.

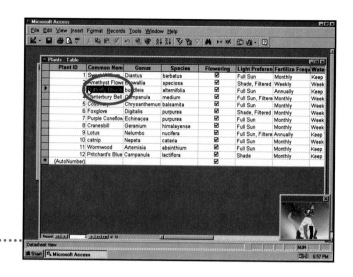

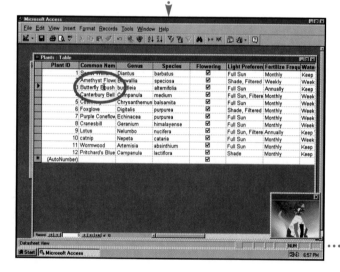

2 Place the mouse pointer between the two "b"s in Bbush, and click once. You see the insertion point is placed between these two letters. (The entire cell text is not selected.)

3 Press the **Delete** key once. This will delete the single "b" to the right of the insertion point.

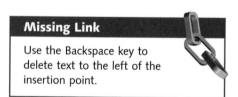

Missing Link

Use the Backspace key to delete text to the left of the insertion point.

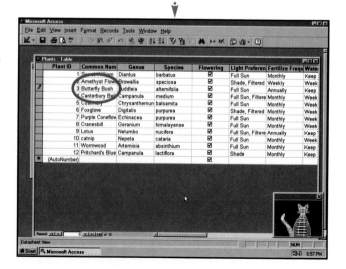

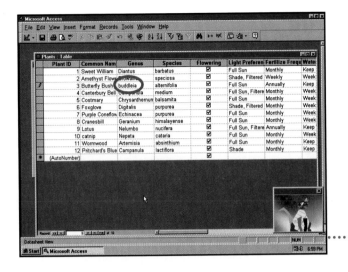

4 Press the **Tab** key to move to the **Genus** field in the same record, and press the **F2** key and the insertion point will be displayed at the right end of the field's value.

Missing Link

The F2 key acts as a toggle between edit and navigation modes. When in the normal table navigation mode, the arrow keys will move you from cell-to-cell. In edit mode, the right- and left-arrow keys will move the insertion point back-and-forth within the cell.

5 Press the **Home** key to move the insertion point to the beginning of the cell value, and press the **Delete** key to remove the letter "b." Now type **B** to correct the entry, making its capitalization consistent with the rest of your records. ■

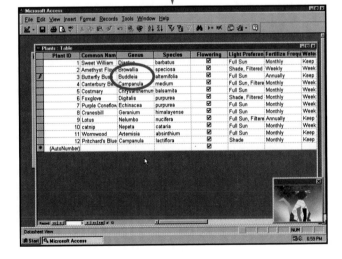

Missing Link

Information can be edited in most cells at any time. You can't edit or enter a value in a field that uses the AutoNumber data type.

Undoing an Edit

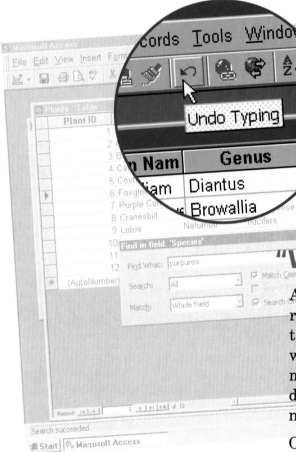

"Why would I do this?"

As you make changes in the fields of a record, you may find that you accidentally made a change to a field in the wrong record. Access allows you to undo many of the changes that you make to data in a record—so long as you have not moved the cursor from the field.

Once you move the cursor from one field to the next, you can undo all changes made to the current record, but not from just a specific field. Once you move the cursor from the record that you are working in and begin editing another record, you won't be able to undo any of your edits.

The only way to change an incorrectly written piece of data would be to edit it again.

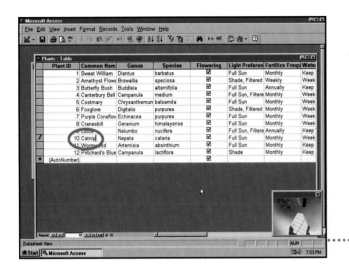

1 Press the arrow keys, moving the cursor to plant number 10 in the **Common Name** column. This uncapitalized entry is inconsistent with the other records in this table. The entire value is automatically selected, type **Catnip**. This action both deletes the original entry and replaces it with the text you enter.

2 Click the **Undo** button on the toolbar. You will see Access undo your editing, and the information returns to its original form.

> **Puzzled?**
>
> You can also undo changes by selecting the Edit, Undo command from the menu. The Undo option itself will vary in its wording depending on what you are doing.

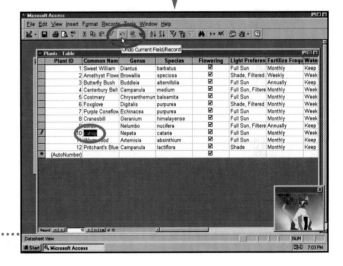

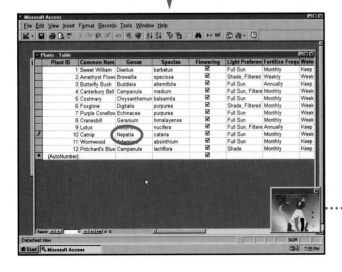

3 Type **Catnip** once again. Press the **Tab** key to move to the next field of this same record and type **Nepetia**, another spelling of this genus that you believe you've seen in a reference book.

101

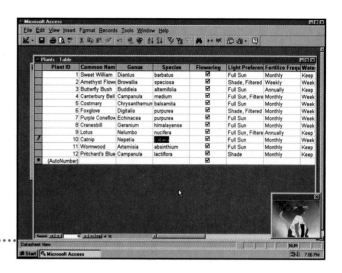

4 Press the **Tab** key once again to move to the next field, cataria. After checking another reference book, which agrees with your first spelling for the genus of the Catnip plant, you decide to reverse all of the changes you have made to this record.

5 Click the **Undo** button and Access reverses *all* of the changes that you have made in this entire record back to the original information. ■

Puzzled?

Once you save a record by moving the cursor to another record, you can still undo the changes by clicking the Undo button, or selecting Edit, Undo Saved Record command from the menu, or by pressing Ctrl+Z. Once you begin to edit another record, you can't recover the previous original record again.

Searching for Information

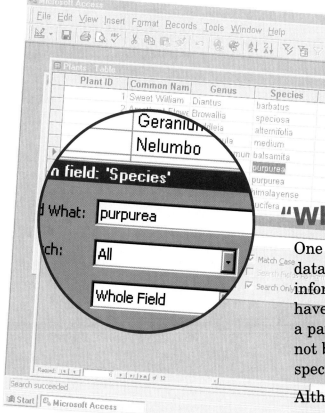

"Why would I do this?"

One of the most powerful features of a database is the ability to find specific information very quickly. How often have you tried to find information about a particular customer or product, and not been able to put your hands on the specific data that you need?

Although Access automatically sorts your records by the value contained in the primary key field, you can quickly search any field for a specified value. In a table with many records, it is much easier to use the Find command than to scroll through the records and risk missing the information that you are searching for. Access enables you to use the Find or Replace commands only on an open table or form.

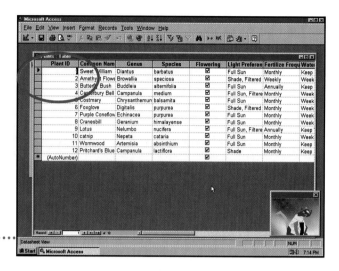

1 Open the **Plants** table if it is not already open.

2 Click the mouse pointer in the **Species** field of the first record in the Plants table, the species barbatus. This is the field that you will search.

Missing Link

Access can search through an entire table instead of just a single field, but this can take much longer in a large table. Whenever possible, try to limit the search to the specific field where you believe the information is located.

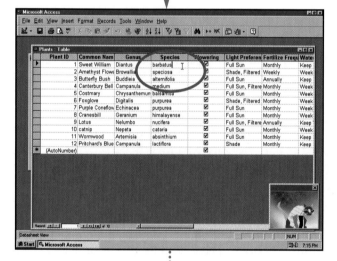

3 Click the **Find** button on the toolbar. The Find dialog box is used to tell Access what you want to search for. As a reminder, Access displays the selected field in the title bar: Find in field: 'Species'.

Puzzled?

You can also use the keyboard shortcut **Ctrl+F**, or the **Edit**, **Find** command to open the Find dialog box.

4 Type what you want Access to search for in the Find What text box. Type **purpurea** in the text box. When you enter something into the text box, the Find First button becomes active.

5 If you aren't sure in which field the item you are looking for will be located, select **All** from the Search combo box. You can also search **Up** the table from the cursor's current location (toward record number 1), or choose to search **Down** the table to the last record.

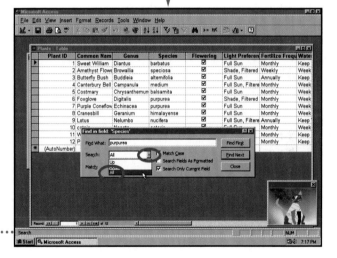

6 In the Match combo box, click the down arrow and choose **Whole Field**.

Missing Link

Access searches the field for exactly what you have entered when the default option **Whole Field** is selected. Select **Any Part of Field** to display matches where your text occurs anywhere in a field, or choose **Start of Field** to display any entry which matches your sample at the beginning of a field value.

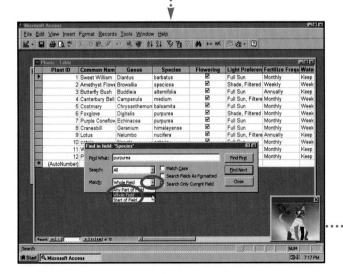

105

7 Click the **Match Case** check box to select only those records which exactly match the value you entered in the Find What text box. With this option selected, Access would find a record with "purpurea," but not "Purpurea." With this box unselected, Access would find any record, including: purpurea, Purpurea, PURPUREA.

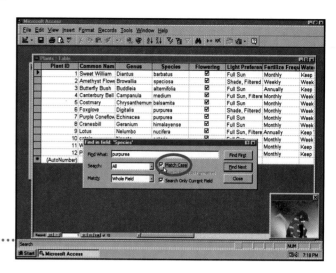

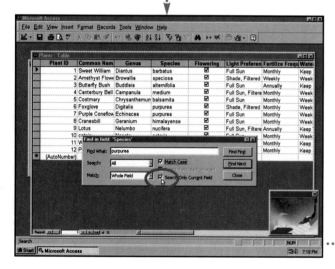

8 The **Search Only Current Field** option is selected by default when the cursor is located in the field to be searched. If you want to search through the entire table, deselect this option. Remember, it will take more time to search through the entire table than it will a single field.

9 Click the **Find First** button to begin the search. After a few seconds, Access will display the first record that meets the criteria you set in the Find dialog box.

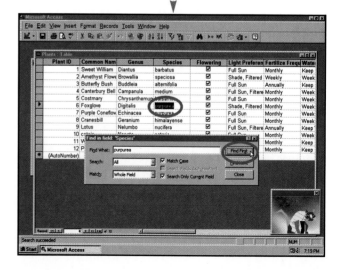

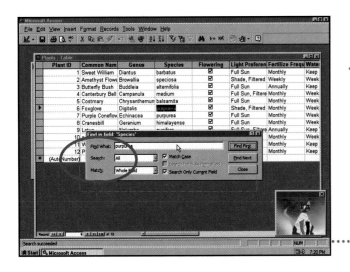

10 Notice how Access moves the record selector indicator from record 1 to a new record. Click and drag the Find dialog box's title bar down if it is preventing you from viewing the found record. As you can see, this record does match your search criteria.

11 Click the **Find Next** button to see if any other records meet your criteria. The record selector again moves down the table to another record.

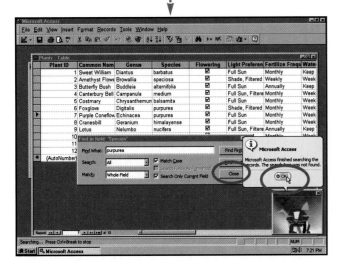

12 Click the **Find Next** button once again. You will now see a new dialog box telling you that Access has finished searching through the table and no other records contain matching values. Click the **OK** button to close this dialog box and then click the **Close** button to close the Find dialog box. ■

Missing Link

If Access doesn't find what you enter in the Find What text box, try changing some of the settings in the Find dialog box, or the search criteria itself.

Replacing Selected Information

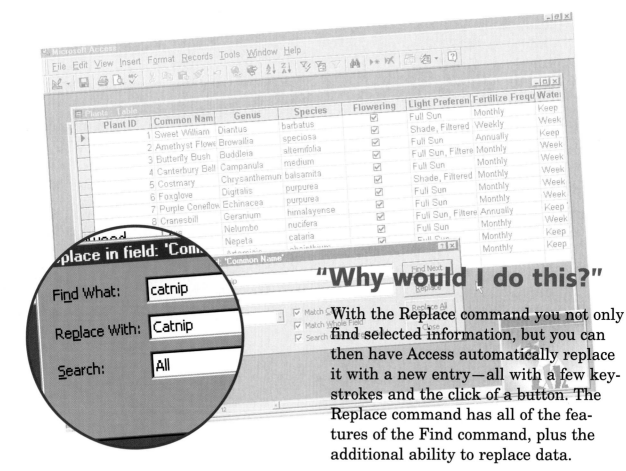

"Why would I do this?"

With the Replace command you not only find selected information, but you can then have Access automatically replace it with a new entry—all with a few keystrokes and the click of a button. The Replace command has all of the features of the Find command, plus the additional ability to replace data.

This can be especially helpful if you accidentally misspell a city name throughout a table, or when for example, the phone company changes an area code—use the Replace command to find and replace just the area codes for selected phone numbers.

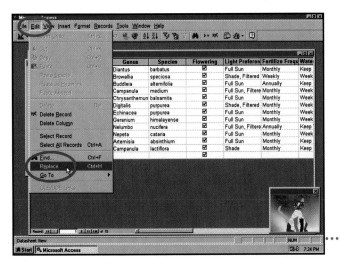

1 Click the mouse pointer on the first record in the **Common Name** field. Remember, you have not re-edited the entry for "catnip" to "Catnip" after undoing your changes on the record. Open the **Edit** menu and click **Replace**.

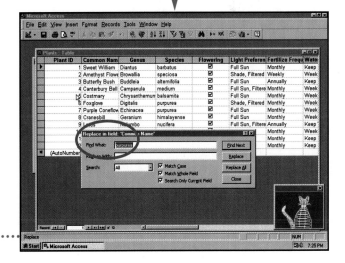

2 The Replace dialog box is displayed. This dialog box displays the field "Common Name" in the title bar, and the text you entered last in the Find dialog box is displayed in the Find What text box. Access assumes that the last item searched for is what you want to replace.

3 Click in the **Find What** text box and type **catnip**. When you enter text in this text box, Access overwrites the previously selected entry.

4 Press the **Tab** key to move to the Replace With text box. Type **Catnip** into this text box.

Missing Link

Similar to the **Find** dialog box, you can use the options available in the Replace dialog box to tell Access where to search in the table and whether to search only for records that exactly match what you have entered. See Task 29 for more information about these options.

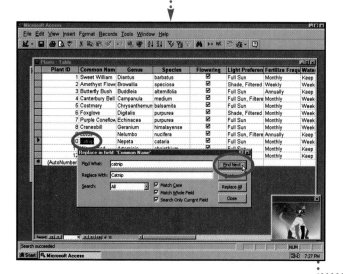

5 Click the **Find Next** button. Access begins the search for the text you have entered in the Find What text box. When Access finds a match, the record selector moves to that record and highlights the field.

Missing Link

If Access doesn't find any matches, try entering the find criteria in a slightly different way, or deselecting the Match Case or Match Whole Field options. Deselecting these options enables Access to expand the search.

6 This is the item that you want to replace, so click the **Replace** button. See how Access changes the field's text to match the text entered in the Replace With text box. If there is another instance of the same item that you want to search for, click the **Find Next** button again. Click the **Close** button to close the Replace dialog box. ■

Missing Link

If you are sure you want all instances of a field changed, use the **Replace All** button.

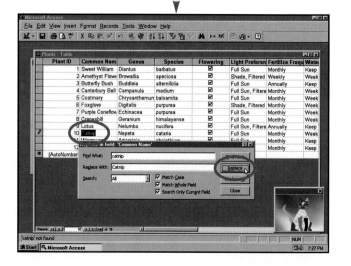

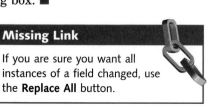

Sorting Records

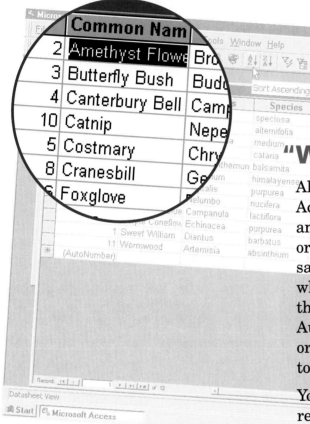

Common Nam	
2	Amethyst Flowe	Bro
3	Butterfly Bush	Budd
4	Canterbury Bell	Cam
10	Catnip	Nepe
5	Costmary	Chry
8	Cranesbill	Ge
6	Foxglove	

"Why would I do this?"

Almost all tables that you create in Access will have a primary key field, and the records in the table will be ordered on this field. This is not necessarily the best way to view records when scrolling through a table. Often the primary key is a field using an AutoNumber data type, and so is ordered in numerical order—smallest to largest.

You have the ability to temporarily resort the records contained in a table by any field. You can choose to sort records in an ascending or a descending order. For example, you can choose to resort your Plants table by the plants Common Name field in an ascending order, which for this field would be the same as an alphabetical order. This would be a much easier way to scroll through the table looking for specific plants.

1 Move the cursor to the **Common Name** field by clicking the mouse pointer in the column. It does not matter which record you place the cursor in.

Puzzled?

Remember, you can move from one field to the next by pressing either the Tab key or the arrow keys.

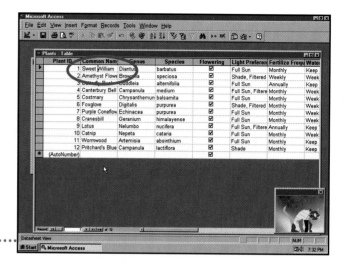

2 Click the **Sort Ascending** button on the toolbar. You will now see the Plants table sorted in alphabetical order by common name. If this field included numeric information, the sort order would look like this: -1, 0, 1, 2, A, b, C, d, . . . y, Z.

Missing Link

Both the Sort Ascending and Sort Descending options are also located on a shortcut menu which is displayed when you right click your mouse.

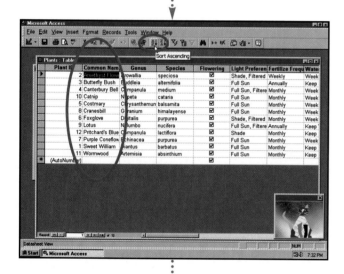

3 Now click the mouse pointer on the **Plant ID** column and click the **Sort Ascending** button once again. You will now see the table in its original order. ■

Puzzled?

Once you close a table that has a primary key field, such as the Plant ID field, Access will automatically order the table by it. When you open the table the next time, it will be in order based on the primary key.

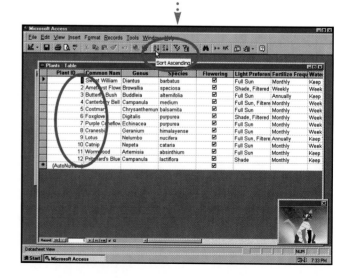

Using Filters

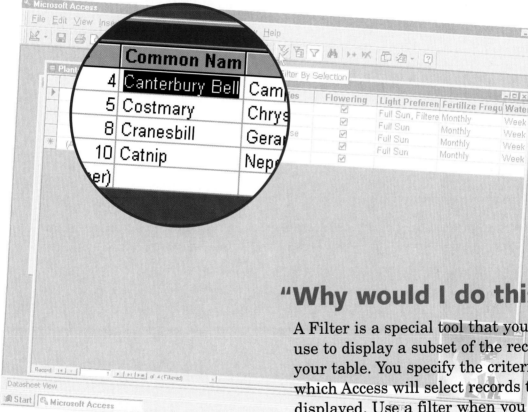

"Why would I do this?"

A Filter is a special tool that you can use to display a subset of the records in your table. You specify the criteria by which Access will select records to be displayed. Use a filter when you want to temporarily view or edit only records that can be selected as a group.

For example, you could filter your Plants table to display only those plants beginning with the letter "B," or which have "Blue" flowers. Filters can be especially helpful when you don't want to work with a large mass of information. In this task, we will filter for all plants whose common name begins with the letter "C."

Task 31: Using Filters

1 Place the mouse pointer on the left of the "C" in Costmary and drag over the "C." This selects the letter "C."

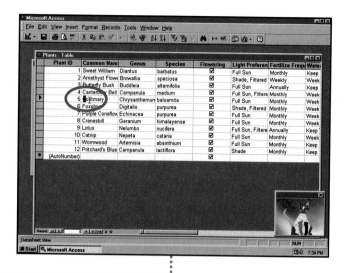

Missing Link

If your mouse is giving you a hard time selecting a single letter you can also select it from your keyboard. Click to the left of the letter "C" and then press and hold the **Shift** key and then press the right-arrow key once. This will select the letter.

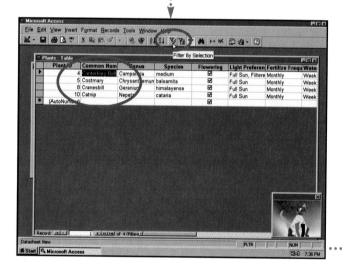

2 Click the **Filter By Selection** button. You will now see only the four plants which have common names beginning with the letter "C."

3 Click the **Apply Filter** button to remove the filter and display all of the records in the table. ■

Missing Link

The Filter By Form button allows you to filter by more than one criteria, such as, name and flower color.

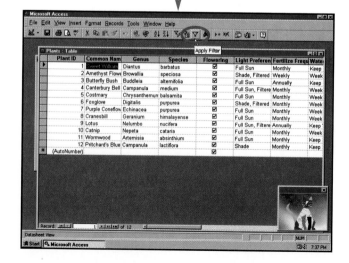

Filtering by Form

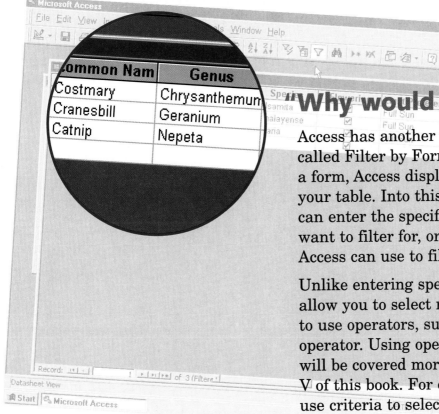

"Why would I do this?"

Access has another method of filtering called Filter by Form. When filtering by a form, Access displays a blank view of your table. Into this blank table, you can enter the specific values that you want to filter for, or use criteria that Access can use to filter for records.

Unlike entering specific values, criteria allow you to select ranges of values or to use operators, such as the LIKE operator. Using operators and criteria will be covered more fully later in Part V of this book. For example, you can use criteria to select all plant records whose common name begins with the letter "c" and that require full sun. This example uses two criteria for filtering records.

Filters can be saved with the table so that they can be used again at a later time. When you save a filter, it isn't displayed like a table on the database window. Filters are specific to the table that they were created for.

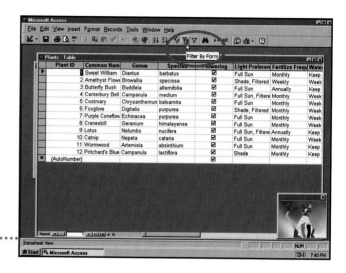

1 Open the **Plants** table and then click the **Filter by Form** button on the toolbar. Access will display a blank view of the Plants table.

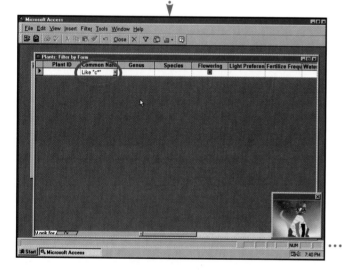

2 Click in the Common Name field and type **Like "c*"** as the first criteria. This tells Access to filter for all records whose common name begins with the letter c and has any number of following letters.

3 Click in the **Light Preference** field and click the arrow button to display the drop-down menu.

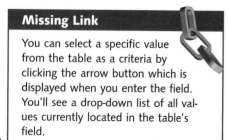

Missing Link

You can select a specific value from the table as a criteria by clicking the arrow button which is displayed when you enter the field. You'll see a drop-down list of all values currently located in the table's field.

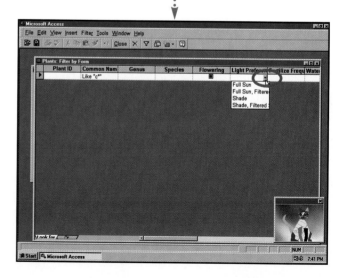

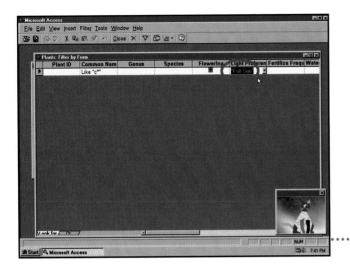

4 Select **Full Sun** from the list. This will be the second criteria that a record must meet before it will be filtered into our results set.

5 Display the results set for this filter by clicking the **Apply Filter** button on the toolbar. This button has a picture of a funnel on it. Once the filtered results set is displayed, the toolbar will change again, moving the button farther to the right and its name will change to Remove Filter.

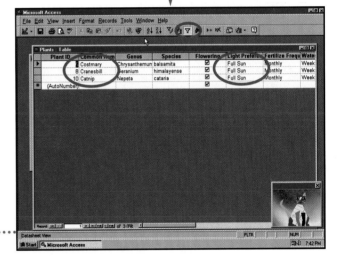

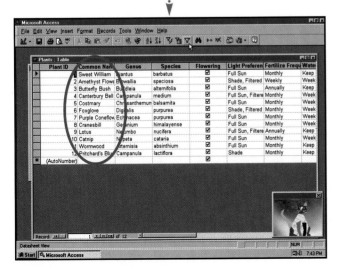

6 Display all of the records in the Plants table once again by clicking the **Remove Filter** button. ■

Missing Link

When you next close the Plants table, you'll be prompted by the Office Assistant to save the changes you have made to the table. The changes include the addition of a filter. If you choose Yes, the filter will be saved with the table so that you can use it again. Choosing No will remove the filter.

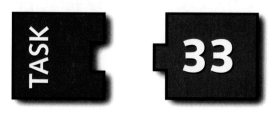

Deleting a Selected Record

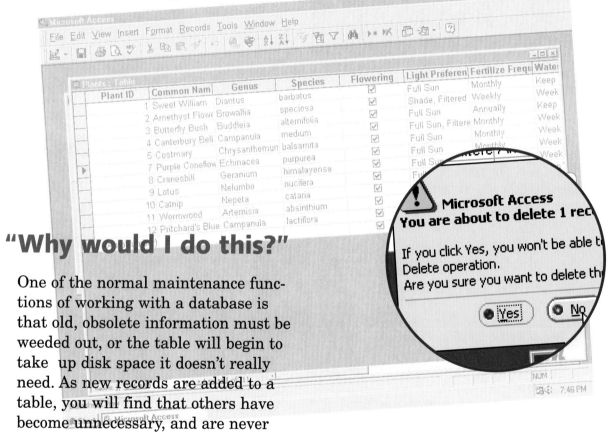

"Why would I do this?"

One of the normal maintenance functions of working with a database is that old, obsolete information must be weeded out, or the table will begin to take up disk space it doesn't really need. As new records are added to a table, you will find that others have become unnecessary, and are never referred to.

For example, you may have records for a customer who no longer buys from you, or a discontinued inventory item, or, in the case of the Plants table, a certain plant you no longer grow. When this occurs, you may want to delete these records from the table.

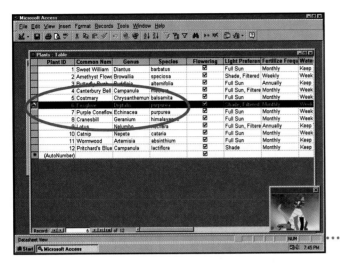

1 Place the mouse pointer on the selector box for plant number 6, Foxglove. Notice how the mouse pointer changes shape to a right-facing arrow. Click the mouse once.

Puzzled?

You can deselect a record by clicking the mouse in any field.

2 Press the **Delete** key and Foxglove is removed. The Office Assistant balloon tells you that you are about to delete a record.

Puzzled?

You can also use the Edit, Cut command on the menu, the Cut button on the toolbar, or the Delete Record option on the shortcut menu. Access places a copy on the Windows Clipboard, enabling you to recover the record.

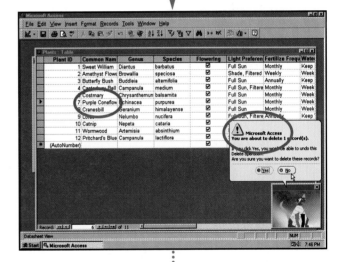

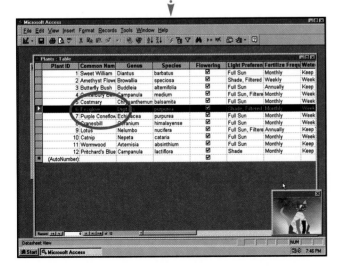

3 Click the **No** option button, so that this record is not deleted. Access replaces the record back into its original position. You would click the Yes option button to remove the record forever. ∎

Resizing Rows and Columns

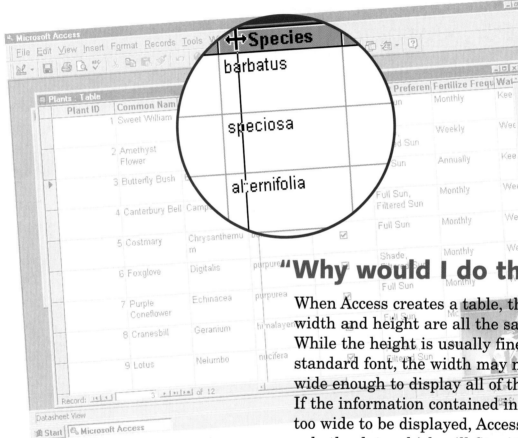

"Why would I do this?"

When Access creates a table, the row width and height are all the same. While the height is usually fine for the standard font, the width may not be wide enough to display all of the text. If the information contained in a field is too wide to be displayed, Access shows only the data which will fit within the column. The rest of the data is still there, but is hidden from view.

You can easily expand or contract the width of a column, or increase and decrease the height of a row. Changing the row height enables you to display the text in a field in two rows, add more white space between records, or display the records in a larger font.

1 You can easily change the height of your rows by placing the mouse pointer between any two row selector buttons. You will see the mouse pointer change shape to resemble a horizontal line with up- and down-arrows.

2 Drag down. This will increase the height of the row. Notice the dark line extending from the mouse pointer across the table. This line indicates what the new height of your row will be once you release the mouse.

Puzzled?

Access doesn't automatically adjust the size of the font. If you decrease the height of the row too much, you records will appear to overlap one another.

3 Release the mouse button. You now see the row height increased to your new setting.

Missing Link

By increasing the row height, you add additional white space to the records, giving the table a less cramped appearance. Changing the height of one row changes all rows in the table.

4 Chrysanthemum has dropped its final "m." Move the mouse pointer to the dividing line between the **Genus** and **Species** field labels. The mouse pointer again changes shape.

Missing Link

Always use the label for the column whose width you want to change, by selecting the dividing line on its right side.

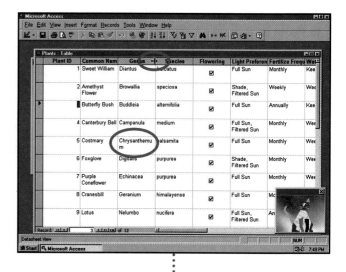

5 Drag the column to the right, increasing the width of the column. You will see a solid line extend from the mouse pointer to the bottom of the table, indicating the column width.

Puzzled?

The height of a row, or the width of a column only affect the appearance of the table, not its underlying data.

6 Release the mouse button to set the column's new width. Notice that Access automatically adjusts the text in the column by moving the letter "m" back up with the rest of the word. Click the **Close** button, but be sure to not save the revised table layout by clicking the **No** button on the Office Assistants balloon. ■

Missing Link

Changes to a column's width affect only the one column, unlike changing a row's height.

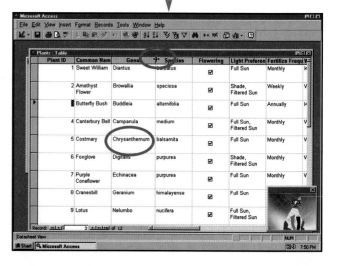

Freezing and Unfreezing Columns

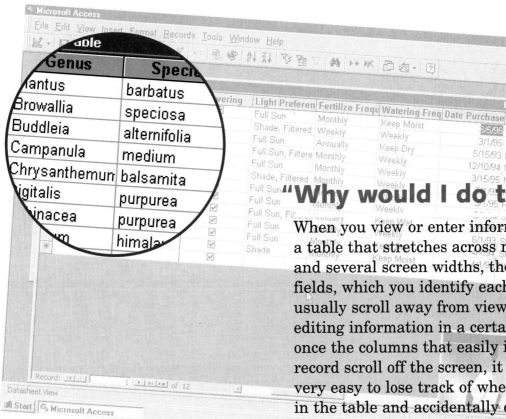

"Why would I do this?"

When you view or enter information in a table that stretches across many fields and several screen widths, the first few fields, which you identify each record by, usually scroll away from view. When editing information in a certain record, once the columns that easily identify a record scroll off the screen, it could be very easy to lose track of where you are in the table and accidentally edit the wrong record.

Access allows you to freeze selected columns so that they remain at the left-most position of your table at all times. As you scroll through your table, this reference field(s) always remains visible to you.

Task 35: Freezing and Unfreezing Columns

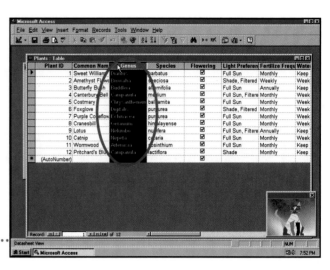

1 Place the mouse pointer on the **Genus** column label. When the mouse pointer changes shape to a downward facing arrow, click it to select the entire column.

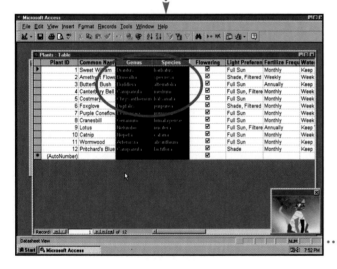

2 Press the keyboard combination **Shift+right-arrow** to select the **Species** column also.

Puzzled?

You can also choose multiple adjacent fields by clicking on the first column label, and dragging across to the last field you want to select.

3 Select **Format** from the menu, and then **Freeze Columns** from the drop-down menu.

Missing Link

If you are freezing a single column, you can select the column and display the shortcut menu at the same time by placing the mouse pointer on the column label and right-clicking your mouse.

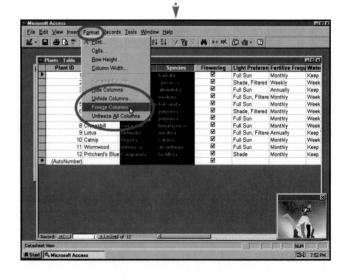

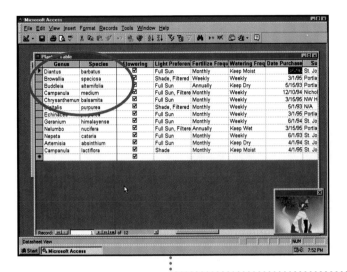

4 The Genus and Species columns remain "frozen" on the far left of your database table. Press the **Tab** key, or use the horizontal scroll bar at the bottom of the table window, to scroll through your table. Notice that Access displays a solid black line between the frozen columns and the unfrozen columns. As you scroll through the fields, you will see the frozen columns remain in place as the other columns scroll across the remaining part of the window.

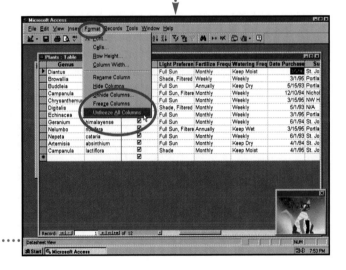

5 Select **Format** from the menu, and then choose **Unfreeze All Columns** from the drop-down menu. Access removes the solid dividing line and restores the table to normal scrolling—all columns moving—but doesn't shift the columns to their original positions.

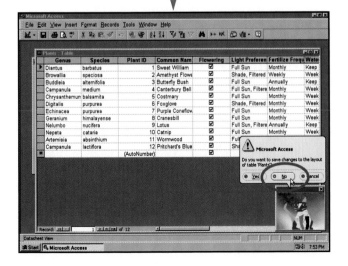

6 Click the **Close** button on the table window, and then the **No** button on the Office Assistants balloon asking you if you want to save your new table layout. ■

Missing Link

You don't have to select the current leftmost column as one of those to freeze in place; you can choose any field(s) which are adjacent to each other.

Hiding and Unhiding Columns

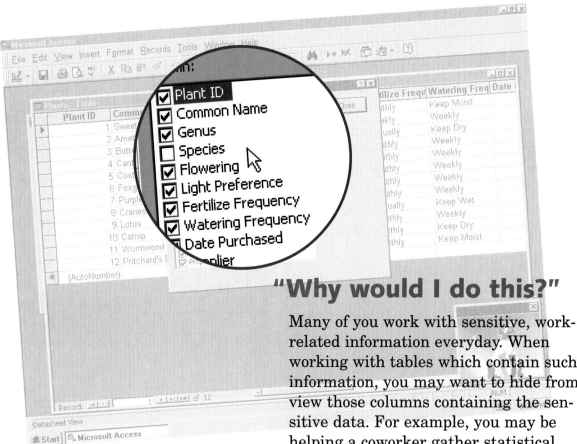

"Why would I do this?"

Many of you work with sensitive, work-related information everyday. When working with tables which contain such information, you may want to hide from view those columns containing the sensitive data. For example, you may be helping a coworker gather statistical information about employee salaries, but you don't want your coworker to see how much money each particular individual makes. If you hide identifying fields, such as First and Last Name, you can decrease the risk of revealing confidential information.

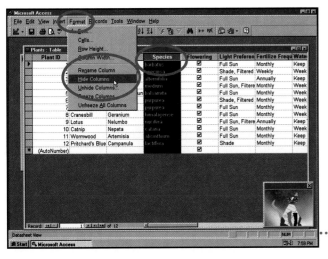

1 Move the cursor to any record in the column that you want to hide and select it, such as the **Species** column. Select **Format** from the menu and then the **Hide Columns** option.

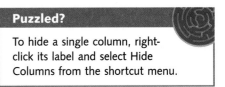

Puzzled?

To hide a single column, right-click its label and select Hide Columns from the shortcut menu.

2 Access immediately hides the column which had the cursor located within it from view.

Puzzled?

You can also hide any number of adjacent columns, by first selecting them and then selecting Format, Hide Columns from the menu.

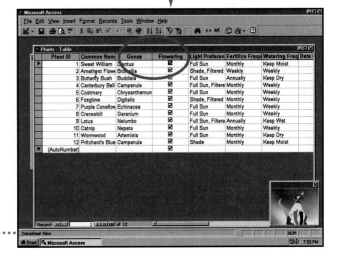

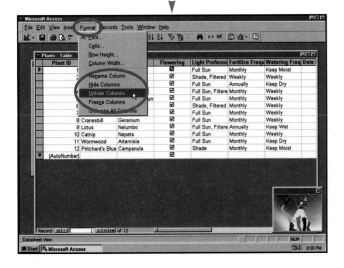

3 To unhide the hidden columns, select **Format** from the menu, and then choose **Unhide Columns** from the drop-down menu. The Unhide Columns dialog box will be displayed.

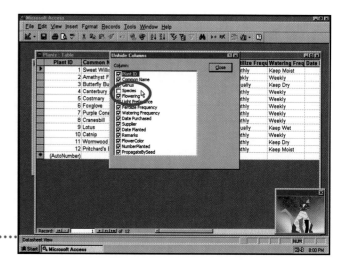

4 Notice that the Species column, which is currently hidden, doesn't have a checkmark in the box beside it. Click the check box. You will see the table blink behind the dialog box as Access unhides the Species column.

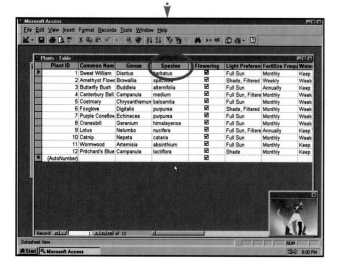

5 Click the **Close** button to return to the table. See how the Species column is now displayed in its normal position. ■

Missing Link

The Unhide Columns dialog box can be used to hide columns which aren't adjacent to each other by selecting Format, Unhide Columns from the menu, and then removing the checkmarks for those columns you wish to hide.

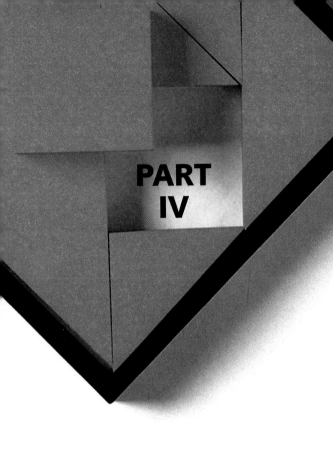

PART IV

Using Database Forms

37 Using the New Object Autoform

38 Building a Form with a Wizard

39 Opening the Form Design View Window

40 Adding Fields to a Form

41 Creating Labels and Entering Text

42 Using a Combo Box

43 Adding a List Box

44 Moving Groups of Objects

45 Editing a Label

46 Using an Option Button

47 Adding Pop-Up Tip Text to Fields

48 Saving Your New Form

49 Opening a Form

50 Entering and Editing Information with a Form

51 Changing the Field Order

T HE NEXT ACCESS OBJECT which you will become familiar with is the *form*. A form can be used for many different purposes, including: displaying information from a table, entering new information into a table, editing existing records, displaying calculated values, displaying information from multiple tables, or using a form as a custom switchboard or dialog box.

Most forms that you will use are based on a table. This means that the information displayed or entered in the form comes from or will be added to the table.

A common use of an Access form is to represent a typical form that you now use, so that you can input information directly into the appropriate tables. For example, you can create a sales order form that will allow you to enter an order directly into the computer; the from will also show you current prices and quantities on hand. This form can also display a calculated total for each item, and the order as a whole.

You can create forms using a Design view layout window. This format gives you the greatest control over all aspects of the form. You can customize your form created in the Design view to display only selected fields; you don't have to use all of the fields available in the table or query.

If you don't include a field in a form which is used for adding, or updating information, you won't be able to add or edit information in these fields unless you do so with underlying code. You will have to either add the necessary information in a separate step, or be sure that the information is not necessary. Custom designed forms can include many special features, including: Labels, option buttons, toggle buttons, combo boxes, list boxes and comand buttons.

You can also use a Form Wizard which will ask you a series of questions in dialog boxes. Each Form Wizard dialog provides several options you can select to decide how your form will look and act. You choose from among several predefined styles that help you create an attractive, easy to use form.

You can also choose to use one of three different AutoForms. An AutoForm is a simple form which Access automatically generates using both a predefined format and all of the fields in the selected table or query. There are three AutoForm designs you can select when building a new form, or you can use the New Object AutoForm option. Your AutoForm options are:

- **Columnar** This form style displays all fields in the table in a column with their labels on the left of the field. Multiple columns will be created so that a single record can be displayed in one page.

- **Tabular** The tabular format displays the field labels at the top, with the records shown below. This is similar to the datasheet view except that both the background and foreground are displayed in color, and the records are separated by additional space.

- **Datasheet** The datasheet AutoForm appears just like a normal datasheet with records in rows and labels appearing at the top, and is displayed in the normal datasheet colors and fonts. All fields are displayed in the width specified in the Field Size property.

- **AutoForm button on toolbar** This option displays a form based on the selected table or query. The form is created with a light gray background. Fields and labels are listed in a single column with fields shown in white, sunken boxes and labels to their left. Text for both is black.

TASK **37**

Using the New Object AutoForm

"Why would I do this?"

You can quickly create a form from a currently selected or open object such as a table or query. With just the click of a button, Access will build a simple form based on the selected object.

The New Object button on the toolbar can create a simple AutoForm. Whenever you want to easily view the records from a table, and you don't want to create a new form nor use a datasheet, create a simple AutoForm. This form simply displays all of field labels in a single column on the left side of the page window, and all of the actual fields in a column beside their respective labels. Fields are further distinguished from labels by being displayed in an embedded text box with a white background. If your table or query has too many fields to be displayed in the AutoForm window, a scroll bar will be active on the right side of the window enabling you to scroll through the form.

The AutoForm can be saved for use later, or you can simply discard it and recreate it when needed.

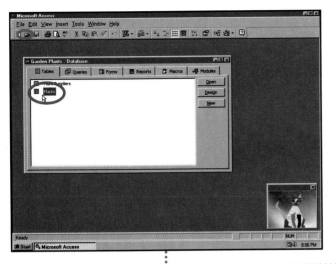

1 Open the **Garden Plants** database and select the **Plants** table. You don't have to open the table, simply select it by clicking it once with the mouse.

Puzzled?

If you opened the Plants table, continue on to the next step. The New Object: AutoForm button works just as well from an open table as it does from one which has simply been selected.

2 Place the mouse pointer on the **New Object** button. If the button's tool tip says **New Object: AutoForm** you can continue to step 3, otherwise click the down-arrow part of the button. The left (icon) side of this two part button activates the currently selected New Object, while the right side (with the down-arrow) displays a drop-down menu of New Objects you can select from. Choose the **AutoForm** option from this list, or click the **AutoForm** button if it has already been selected.

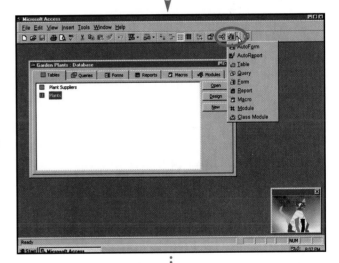

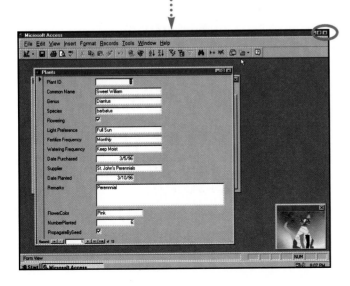

3 After a few seconds you will see the AutoForm for the Plants table appear on your screen. Use the **Page Down** key on your keyboard, or the record navigation buttons at the bottom of the form to view additional records. Click the **Close** (**X**) button and don't save the form when prompted by a dialog box or the Office Assistant. ■

TASK

38

Building a Form with a Wizard

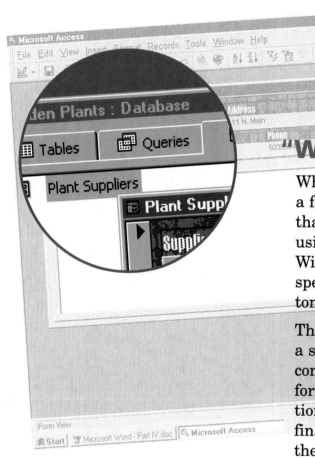

"Why would I do this?"

When you are ready to begin designing a form with more features and controls than a simple AutoForm allows for, try using the Form Wizard. The Form Wizard can help you design a form with special backgrounds, color, and customized field and label styles.

The Form Wizard will take you through a series of dialog boxes, each of which is concerned with a different aspect of the form's design. As you make your selections, they will be compiled into your final form. Once you are finished with the Form Wizard, you can open the form and begin to use it, or you can open it in the Form Design window so you can make additional changes to the form's design. Remember, you can always try the form out first and then refine its design to more closely suit your needs.

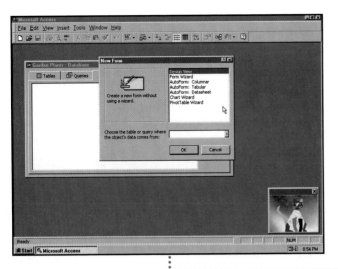

1 Place the mouse pointer on the **Forms** tab button and click once to display the Forms list. Click the **New** button, or press **Ctrl+N**.

Missing Link

As you create new forms, they will be listed here, just as the tables you built were added to the Tables list. The Forms list is empty because you have not created and saved any forms yet.

2 The New Form dialog box is displayed. From the list box, choose the **Form Wizard** option. In the combo box below the list, click the down-arrow to display the list of objects (tables or queries) on which you can base this form. Choose the table **Plant Suppliers**, and then click the **OK** button.

Puzzled?

You can also open the New Form dialog box by selecting the **Insert**, **Form** command from the menu, or clicking the down-arrow button of the New Object button on the toolbar and choosing **Form.**

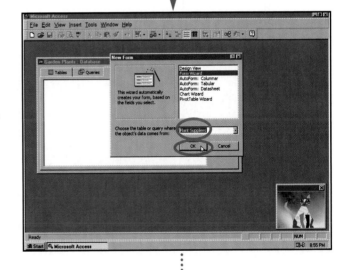

3 You will now see the first of several Form Wizard dialog boxes. Use the Available Field list box to choose those fields to be included on the form. Choose single fields by selecting them and then clicking the > button and thus moving the field from the list box to the Selected Fields list box.

4 Since you want to include all of the fields from the Plant Suppliers table on the new form, click the >> button to place them in the Selected Fields list box. Click the **Next >** button.

Missing Link

If you decide not to include a field, you can always select it in the Selected Fields list box and then click the **<** button to remove it. The **<<** button deselects all selected fields.

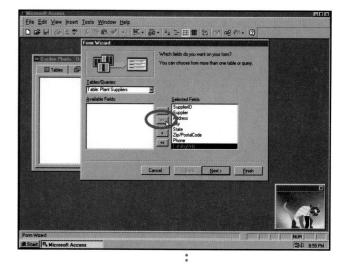

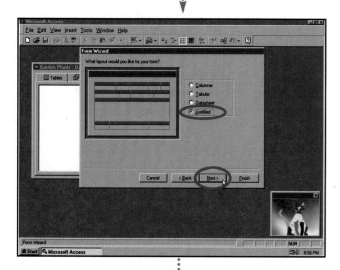

5 You must now choose from four layout options. By clicking an option button, you will see the sample change, giving you a thumbnail view of how your form will be laid out. Click each to view them, and then select the **Justified** option. Click the **Next >** button.

6 This dialog box enables you to select from among ten different background and field/label combination styles. Select the **Pattern** option from the list. Click the **Next >** button.

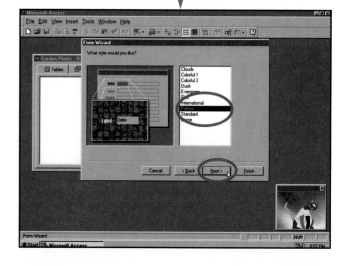

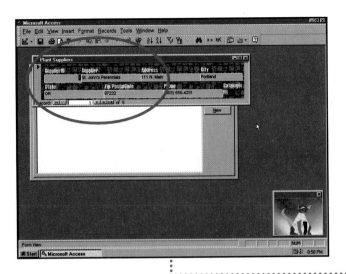

7 In this dialog box you will choose a title for the form. Access enters a default title which is the same as the object on which the form is based. If you don't like the title, just type another in the text box. You can also choose between opening the form ready to enter information, or in Design view so that you can further customize the form. Click the **Finish** button. Access builds the form and displays it.

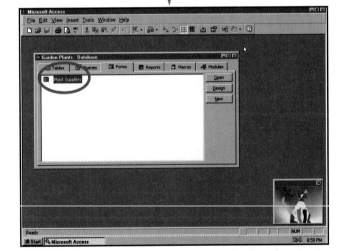

8 You can now enter new records or view existing records (if there are any in the Plant Suppliers table). Close the form by clicking the **Close** (**X**) button in the corner of the form window. You will now see the form listed in the Forms list. Access automatically saves this form when it is built.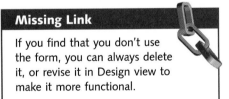

Missing Link

If you find that you don't use the form, you can always delete it, or revise it in Design view to make it more functional.

139

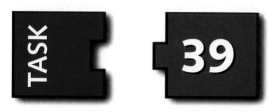

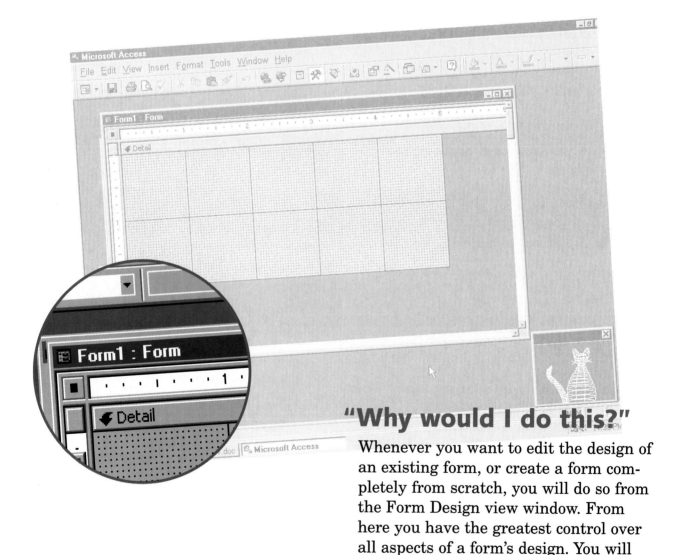

Opening the Form Design View Window

"Why would I do this?"

Whenever you want to edit the design of an existing form, or create a form completely from scratch, you will do so from the Form Design view window. From here you have the greatest control over all aspects of a form's design. You will make all of the decisions about the placement of fields and labels, and the appearance of all objects on the form.

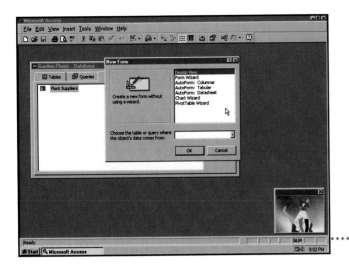

1 From the Database window click the **Forms** tab button, displaying the Forms list. This list shows the Plant Suppliers form which you have already created. Click the **New** button.

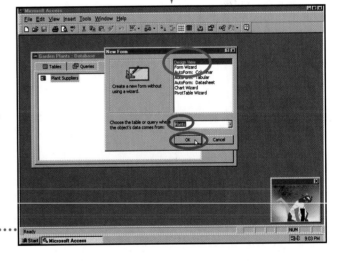

2 The New Form dialog box appears. Select **Design View** from the list, and choose the **Plants** table from the combo box as the base for the form. Click **OK**.

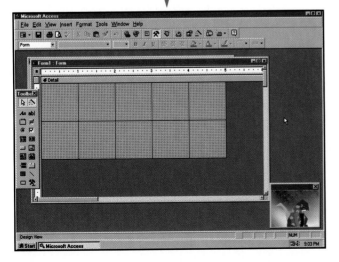

3 The Form Design view window is now displayed for you. From this window you can build your own unique form, as explained in the following tasks. ■

Puzzled?

Access replaces the Standard toolbar with two new toolbars, Form Design and Formatting, and a floating toolbox, which is simply called the Toolbox. You will use the tools available here to help you design your form.

Adding Fields to a Form

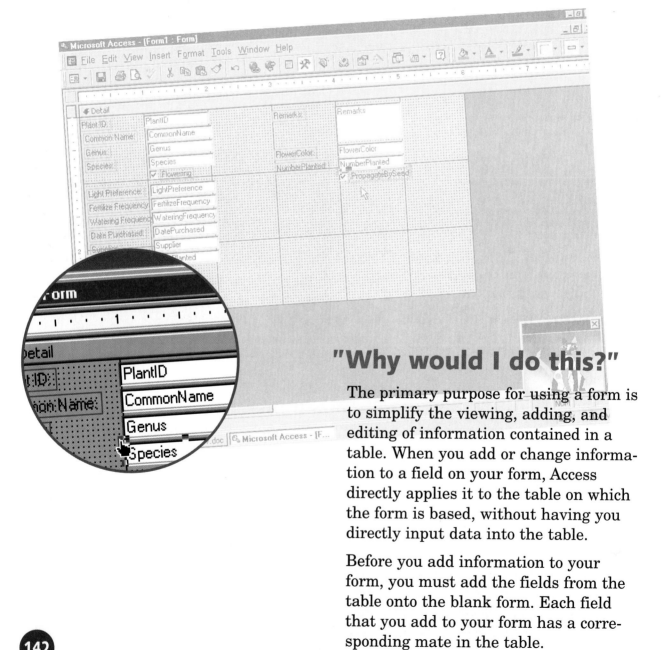

"Why would I do this?"

The primary purpose for using a form is to simplify the viewing, adding, and editing of information contained in a table. When you add or change information to a field on your form, Access directly applies it to the table on which the form is based, without having you directly input data into the table.

Before you add information to your form, you must add the fields from the table onto the blank form. Each field that you add to your form has a corresponding mate in the table.

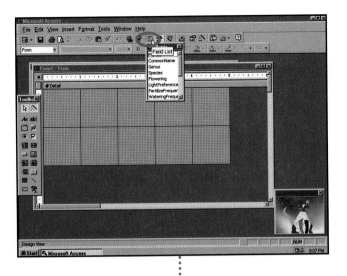

1 Place the mouse pointer on the **Field List** button and click it. You will see a floating list box showing the available fields which you can use on your form.

Puzzled?

As you place each field, you will actually see two boxes added to the form. The right box is the actual field, while the left box is the field label. When you complete the form, the label box still shows the label, while the field box is either blank until you enter data into it, or will display data from the selected record.

2 Click and drag the **Plant ID** field from the Field List box to the Detail area of the form. You see the mouse pointer change shape to represent a field.

Puzzled?

If you have many fields to place, and not very much room in the detail area, click the Maximize button on the form window to increase its size. (The figures in this task have been maximized.) You can also use the scroll bar to move around, but this can be inconvenient.

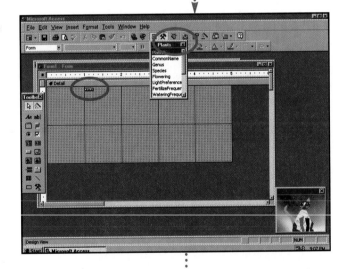

3 Drag the field to the location below the Detail bar and beside the black one-inch line on the horizontal ruler and drop the field by releasing the mouse button.

Missing Link

You can quickly remove the floating list box by either clicking its Close (**X**) button, or by clicking the Field List button on the toolbar again.

4 Both the field and its label can be easily moved once you have placed them on the form grid by moving the mouse pointer to an edge of the field. You'll see the pointer change shape to resemble a hand. Click and drag the field and label to a new position. As you drag the field, its outline moves with you so that you can place it accurately.

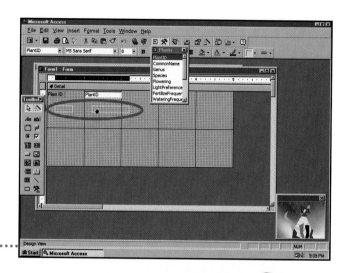

Missing Link

The eight black squares that surround the field box are handles. The largest handle in the upper-left corner is used to move the box independent of its mate while the other seven are used to change the size of the box.

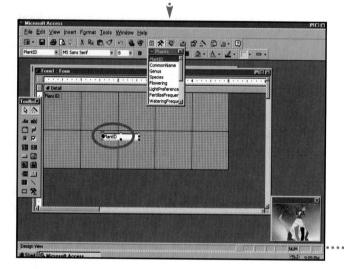

5 Move the mouse pointer to the large handle on the field box and drag it to the new position shown here. Click the **Undo** button to return the field to is original location.

6 Select and drag the field **CommonName** from the field list to the Detail form area, beneath the Plant ID field. Do the same with the fields **Genus** and **Species**.

Missing Link

Use the horizontal and vertical rulers to help estimate the size of the form, and the placement and size of the form's objects.

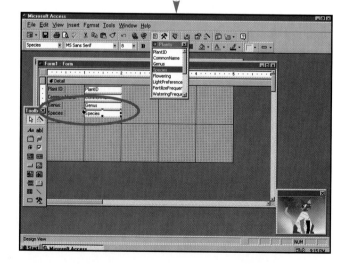

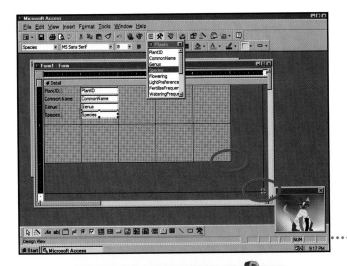

7 You can increase the size of the form grid by dragging the right or bottom edge of the grid, or its lower right corner. Move the mouse to the lower corner of the form grid, you'll see the mouse change shape to a four-headed arrow. Drag the corner down and to the right until the grid is six by three inches.

Missing Link

If you can't see the vertical ruler, simply move the toolbox to a new location by dragging it by the title bar. Dragging one of its edges will change its shape, or you can dock it to one of the edges of the Design window by dragging it there, where it will appear like a standard toolbar.

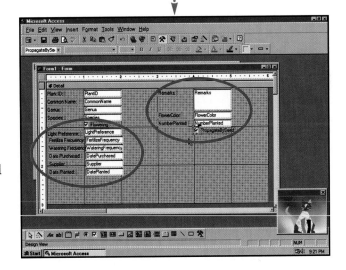

8 Place the remaining fields on the form grid and then click the Close (**X**) button on the Field List box. ∎

Missing Link

Fields which use the Yes/No data type, and have been assigned the Check Box display control will automatically be placed as check boxes on the form. You can change this format.

Missing Link

As you place each field, notice how the dots and lines act like magnets to attract your fields to the closest part of the grid. This feature is called *Snap to Grid*, helping you to align and adjust your objects that you place on the form.

41

Creating Labels and Entering Text

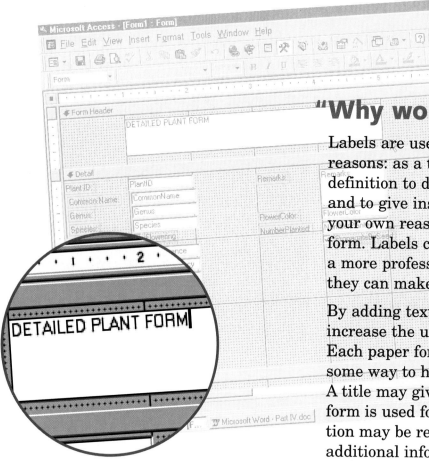

"Why would I do this?"

Labels are used on a form for several reasons: as a title or subtitle, to give definition to different parts of a form, and to give instructions. You may have your own reasons for adding labels to a form. Labels can help to give your form a more professional appearance and they can make your form easier to use.

By adding text as a label, you will increase the usability of your form. Each paper form you see uses text in some way to help the user complete it. A title may give a basic idea of what a form is used for, but additional information may be required. The amount of additional information will vary depending upon your intended user.

For example, you can create a small block label which contains instructions on what is required to complete a sales order. This will help someone who is unfamiliar with the form.

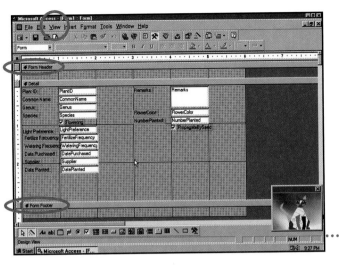

1 Open the **View** menu and choose the **Form Header/Footer** option. You will see two new grid sections added to your form, a header above and a footer below.

Puzzled?

Do not use the Page Header/ Footer option. This option adds a header and footer which is only displayed when the form is printed.

2 Place the mouse pointer at the top edge of the Detail bar. You'll see the pointer change to a bar with arrows. Drag the edge of the Form Header down about $1/2$-inch, increasing the width of the header to about $3/4$-inch.

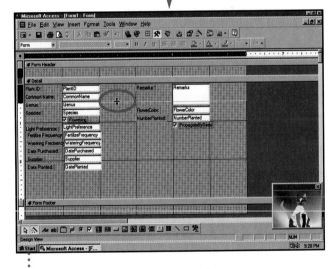

Missing Link

When moving or changing the size of an object on the form grid, notice how a black band is displayed on both the vertical and horizontal rulers, indicating the current size and placement of the object.

3 From the toolbox, select the **Label** button. Place the mouse pointer, which is now in the shape of the letter "A" with a plus sign, on the form header grid. Place the crosshairs, or plus sign, at the location where you want the upper-left corner of your label to begin.

Task 41: Creating Labels and Entering Text

4 Drag diagonally across to the opposite corner where you want the label box to end and release the mouse button. A blank label box now appears with a blinking insertion point inside.

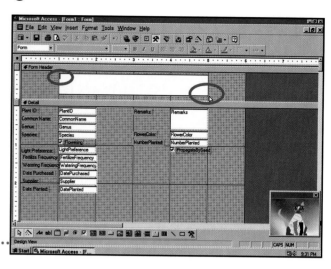

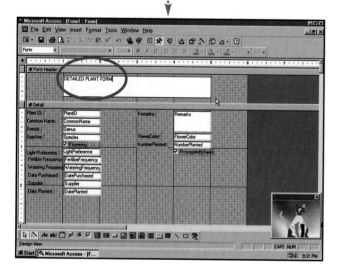

5 Type **DETAILED PLANT FORM** as the title for this form. ■

Puzzled?

If you decide that you don't want to keep a label box, simply select it and press the **Delete** key. If the text doesn't fit within the label box, just select it and then drag one of the resize handles until it is large enough. If you haven't yet entered any text into the label, pressing the **Enter** key will remove the label.

Using a Combo Box

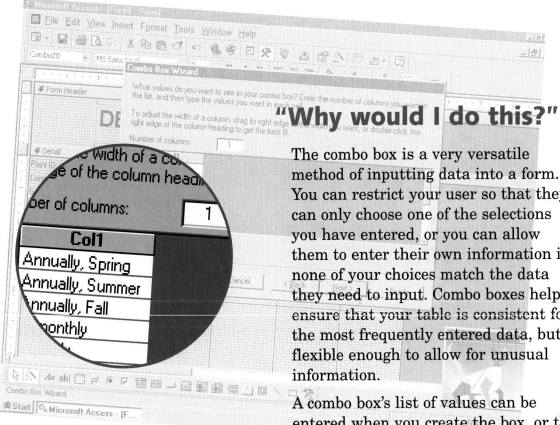

The combo box is a very versatile method of inputting data into a form. You can restrict your user so that they can only choose one of the selections you have entered, or you can allow them to enter their own information if none of your choices match the data they need to input. Combo boxes help ensure that your table is consistent for the most frequently entered data, but flexible enough to allow for unusual information.

A combo box's list of values can be entered when you create the box, or the list can derive from a table or query. If a list doesn't often change, you might create the list of values when you create the combo box. If your list is frequently updated, then base the combo box on a table or query. It is much easier to update a table or run a query, than edit a combo box list. The updates are automatically reflected in the combo box list the next time it is accessed.

Task 42: Using a Combo Box

1 Select the field **FertilizeFrequency** on your form. Remember, select a field by clicking the field text box, not its attached label. Press the **Delete** key.

Puzzled?

If you accidentally select and delete the field's label box, the field box remains on your form. Simply select and delete the field box as a separate step. A field box can exist without its attached label, but the label can't exist without its associated field box.

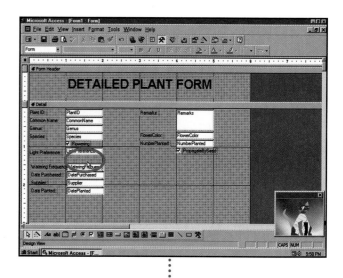

2 Access removes the field from your form, but not from the table. Click the **Control Wizards** button on the toolbox, if it is not already selected,

Puzzled?

If the toolbox is in your way, move it to the other side of the screen, or dock it on the bottom or side of the window by dragging it to a new location.

3 Click the **Combo Box** button. Notice how the Control Wizard and Combo Box buttons now appear depressed. A depressed button is a button that you have selected.

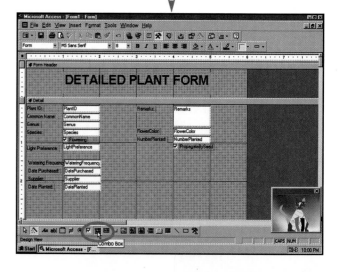

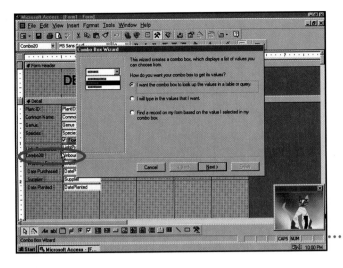

4 The mouse pointer changes to look like a plus sign with the accompanying Combo box. Move the mouse pointer to the position where you want to place the combo box and click.

5 The first of several Combo Box wizard dialog boxes appears. Click the second option button **I will type in the values that I want**, and then click the **Next >** button to move on to the next dialog box.

> ### Missing Link
>
> Remember, you can always use the Back button to go back to a previous dialog box, or use the Cancel button to stop the wizard and close the dialog box. Canceling will leave you with an unbound combo box on your form. You can delete the unbound combo box by selecting it and pressing the **Delete** key.

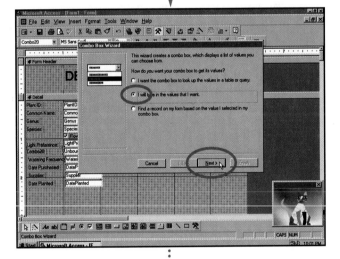

6 Choose the number of columns to be displayed by the combo box. For our example, we only need 1 column. Press the **Tab** key to move from the Number of columns text box to the Col1 area.

> ### Missing Link
>
> The number of columns displayed in the second half of the dialog box is dependent upon the number entered in the Number of columns: text box.

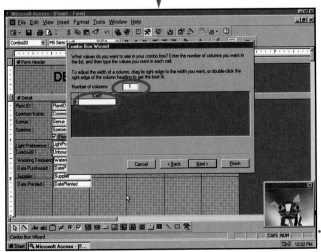

7 Enter the following values, pressing the **Tab** key after each; **Annually**, **Spring**, **Annually**, **Summer**, **Annually**, **Fall**, **Bi-monthly**, **Monthly**, and **Weekly**. You should have six rows now completed. Click the **Next >** button to display the next dialog box.

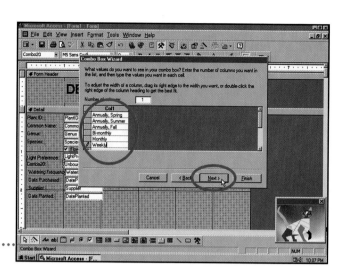

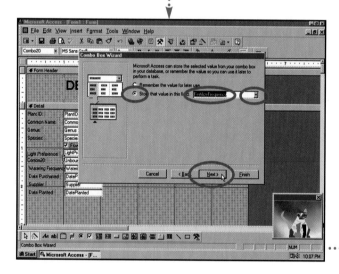

8 This dialog box enables you to decide how the value you select, or enter, will be used. Choose the second option button, **Store that value in this field**. Select the field **FertilizeFrequency** from the combo box list. This is the table field where the selected value will be stored. Click the **Next >** button.

9 Type **Fertilization Frequency** into the text box as the label for the combo box.

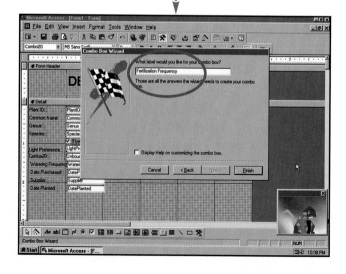

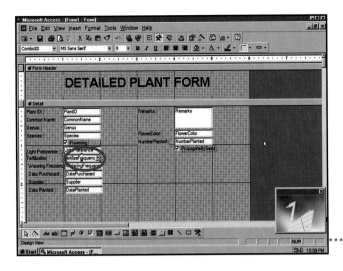

10 Click the **Finish** button. You'll now see the new combo box placed on the form grid.

11 Adjust the size of the combo boxes attached label so that all of the text Fertilization Frequency can be seen. ■

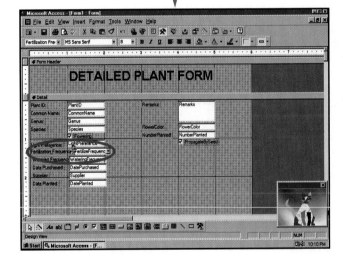

Adding a List Box

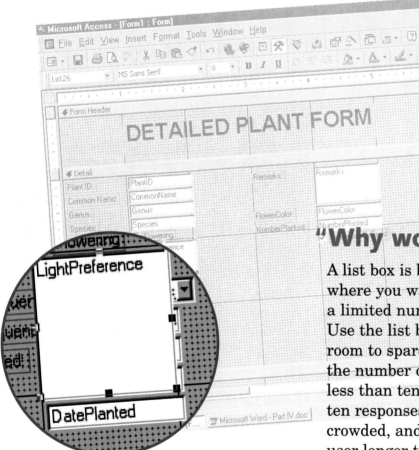

"Why would I do this?"

A list box is best used for those fields where you want to restrict your user to a limited number of valid responses. Use the list box only when you have room to spare on your form, and when the number of valid responses is usually less than ten. If you allow more than ten responses, the list becomes too crowded, and may actually take the user longer to search through the list than it would to simply type an item.

A list box allows the user to type in the first few letters of the value that they want to find, and Access will scroll through the list to find the first matching value. A list box will generally take at least three lines on your form, and if you have room, it can easily take more.

1 Select the **LightPreference** field and press the **Delete** key, removing the field and its attached label from the form grid.

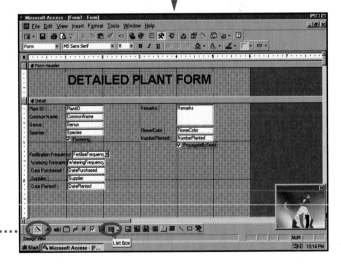

Missing Link

If you select the wrong field, or decide you don't want to delete the field, click the Undo button and Access will immediately place the field back in position. Undo only affects the last entry, so you won't be able to reinsert the field if you have issued another command after deleting the field.

2 Be sure that the **Control Wizards** button is selected, and then click the **List Box** button on the toolbox.

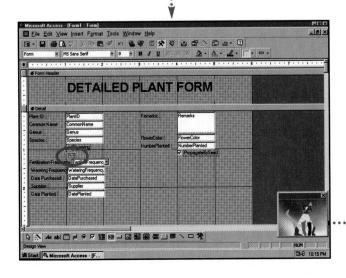

3 Place the mouse pointer, now in the shape of a plus sign and list box, to the place where the LightPreference field was and click the mouse button once. Access inserts a blank field and displays the first List Box Wizard dialog box.

Puzzled?

Access inserts a field with a default size and shape which varies with each type of field. You can resize the field later using its resize handles.

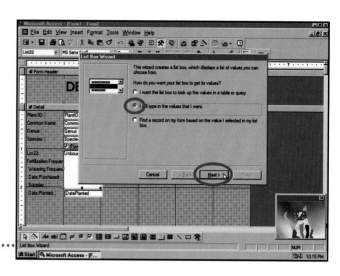

4 Click the second option button, **I will type in the values that I want**, and then click the **Next >** button to move to the next dialog box.

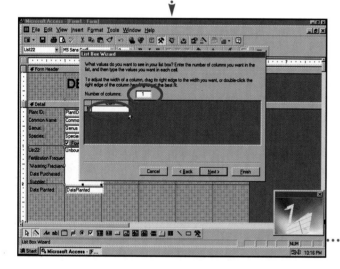

5 The default option—1 column—is fine for this field, so press the **Tab** key to move to the first cell. Remember, you can also select this cell by placing the mouse pointer inside it and clicking.

6 Type **Full Sun** into this first cell and press the **Tab** key to move to the next. Type the following values, pressing the **Tab** key between each; **Filtered Sun**, **Full Shade**, **Partial Shade**, **Morning Sun**, and **Afternoon Sun**. Click the **Next >** button to display the next dialog box.

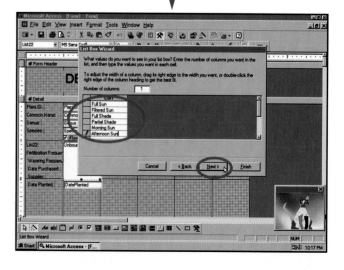

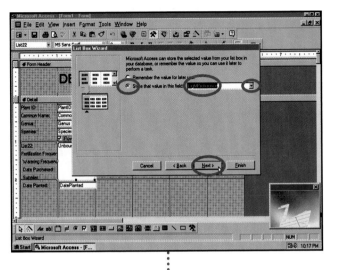

7 Click the second option button, **Store that value in this field** and then select the **LightPreference** field from the combo box beside it. Click the **Next >** button to move to the last dialog box.

Missing Link

Remember, you can use the **< Back** button to return to a previous dialog box if you want to change something.

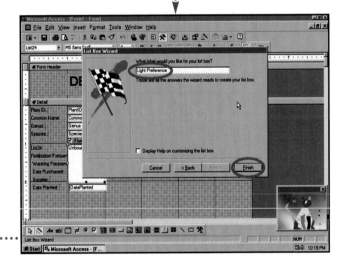

8 Type **Light Preference** into the text box at the top of the dialog box to replace the default label.

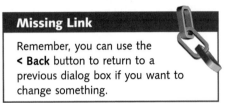

9 Click the **Finish** button. Access will complete the list box and add it to the form. Here the list box is displayed at the default size and shape. ■

Missing Link

In the next task you'll learn how to adjust the default size and shape of a field object.

TASK

44

Moving Groups of Objects

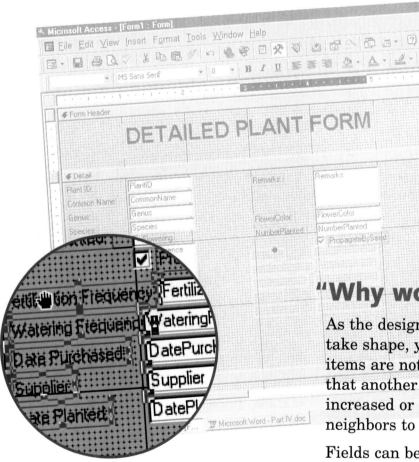

"Why would I do this?"

As the design of your form begins to take shape, you may find that some items are not where they should be, or that another field's size needs to be increased or decreased, causing its neighbors to be out of place.

Fields can be moved one-by-one or you can move them as a group. Moving fields as a group is advantageous because the group members all retain the same relative position to each other. Moving the fields individually means that you have to make sure to properly space the fields yourself. In this task, you will learn to select and move several objects as a group.

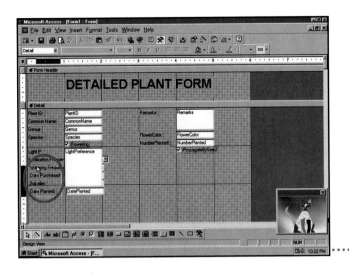

1 Place the mouse pointer on the form grid between the DatePlanted field and its label. Click and drag the mouse up and then to the left until it touches the label box that says **Fertilization** inside. You'll see that Access draws a rectangle from the point you first clicked the mouse to its current location.

2 Let go of the mouse button. You'll see that you have selected all of the field objects and their labels within or touched by the rectangle. Even though the rectangle didn't touch any of the field objects, they have also been selected.

> **Puzzled?**
>
> If you miss a field, just reselect the group, making a larger selection rectangle.

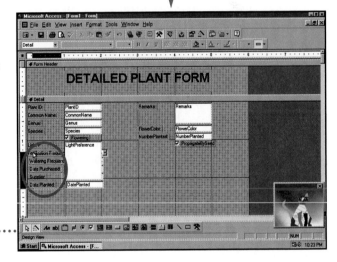

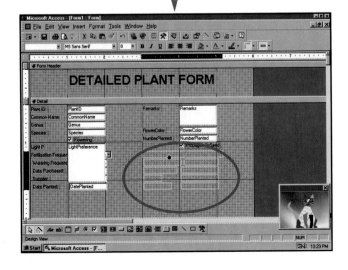

3 Drag these five fields and their attached labels to the right half of the form.

4 Release the mouse button and the fields and labels are dropped in the new location.

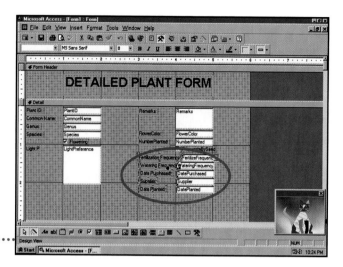

Puzzled?

You can also select objects which aren't adjacent to each other by pressing and holding the **Shift** key on your keyboard while you click each object you want to move.

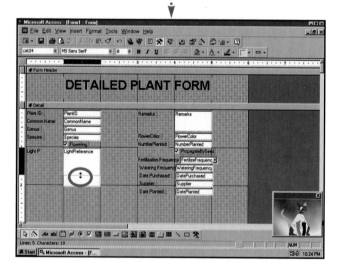

5 Now select the **LightPreference** field and drag its bottom resize handle up until it is approximately $3/4$-inch in height. ■

Missing Link

If your fields end up being slightly to one side or the other, just drag them back into the correct place. This sometimes takes practice, especially if you have a very sensitive mouse.

Editing a Label

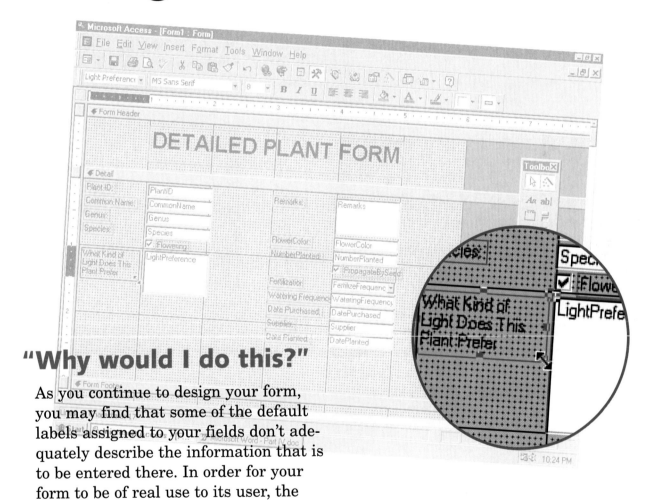

"Why would I do this?"

As you continue to design your form, you may find that some of the default labels assigned to your fields don't adequately describe the information that is to be entered there. In order for your form to be of real use to its user, the user should be able to know what information is required for the field by simply reading its label.

With just a few keystrokes you can change a field's label. In this task, you will change a label's text to quickly tell you what kind of information should be entered.

1 Select the attached label for the **LightPreference** field, which now reads as **Light P**. Resize handles should now appear around the label box. If you look closely, there is also a move-handle located at the upper left corner of the field box; ignore it.

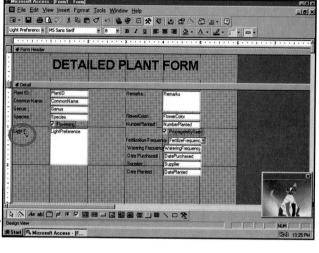

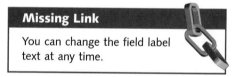

2 Press the **Enter** key to switch to edit mode, and place the insertion point at the end of the label's text. You could also use the standard edit mode key, F2. Press the Backspace key to delete all of the text in the box. Type **What Kind of Light Does This Plant Prefer**. See how the label stretches across the field object to which it belongs. Press the **Enter** key to toggle out of edit mode.

Missing Link

You can change the field label text at any time.

3 Now drag the lower-right corner resize handle to the left and down, so that the lower-right corner is one gridline to the left of the field object. This creates a label text box which holds three lines of text. Resize the label text box until the text fits neatly within it. ■

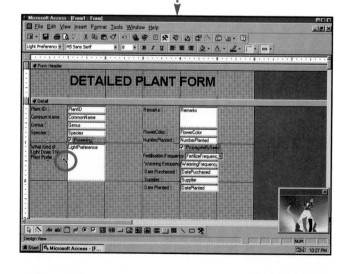

Using an Option Button

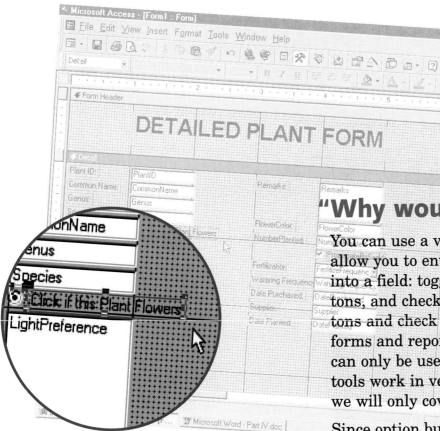

"Why would I do this?"

You can use a variety of tools which allow you to enter a Yes/No response into a field: toggle buttons, option buttons, and check boxes. Both option buttons and check boxes can be used in forms and reports, while toggle buttons can only be used in forms. Each of these tools work in very similar ways, and so we will only cover the option button.

Since option buttons can be grouped with other option buttons, you can create a range of selections, instead of simply a Yes/No. However, creating groups is beyond the scope of this book. Query the Office Assistant for more information about creating an option button group.

In this task, you will create an option button for a Yes/No field.

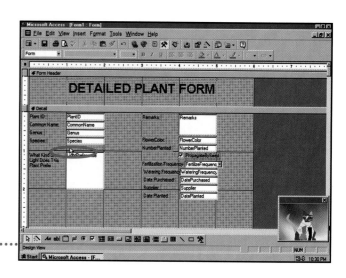

1 Select the **Flowering** field and press the **Delete** key to remove it from the from grid.

2 Click the **Option Button** tool on the toolbox. Move the mouse pointer to the form grid where the Flowering field had been located.

3 Click the mouse button, and you'll now see an option button on the left and a generic label on the right. Option buttons, like check boxes, place the field and label opposite of other objects. Right-click the mouse to display a shortcut menu and select the **Properties** option. Make sure you select the option button and not the label or you will get a different property sheet.

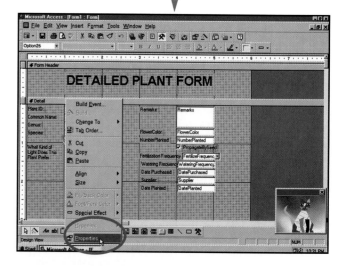

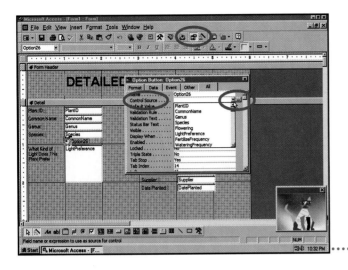

4 The properties sheet for the new option button is displayed. Press the **down-arrow** key on your keyboard, highlighting the Control Source text box. Click the arrow button at the end of the combo box to display a list of available field objects.

5 Select **Flowering** from the list as the field object; this is the field that controls the option button. When you select this button, Access enters a "Yes" response into the Flowering field in the Plants table.

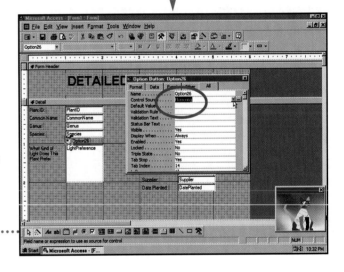

6 Close the properties sheet by clicking its Close (**X**) button.

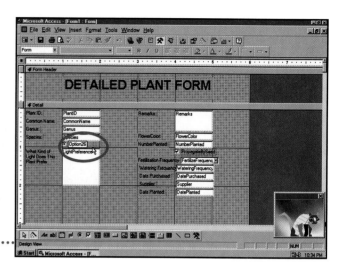

7 Select the option button's attached label and press the **Enter** key, shifting to Edit mode.

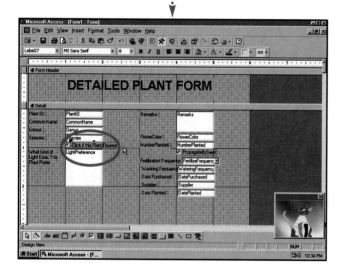

8 Press the Backspace key to delete the existing label and type **Click if this Plant Flowers**, pressing the **Enter** key to toggle back to select mode. ■

Adding Pop-Up Tip Text to Fields

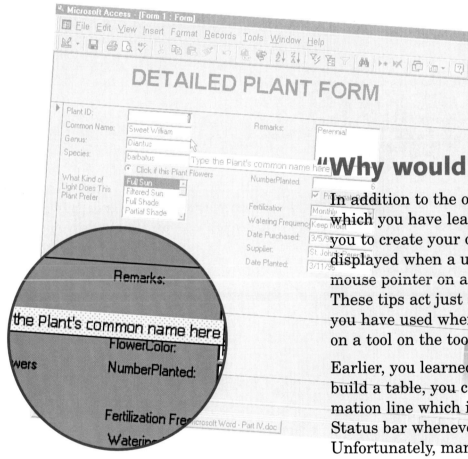

"Why would I do this?"

In addition to the other forms of help which you have learned, Access allows you to create your own pop-up tips to be displayed when a user pauses the mouse pointer on a field in the form. These tips act just as the tool tips that you have used when placing the mouse on a tool on the toolbar.

Earlier, you learned that when you build a table, you can include an information line which is displayed in the Status bar whenever the field is active. Unfortunately, many people don't notice messages in the Status bar, or they may not have activated the field by moving the insertion point to it. By inserting a tip, your user will see a message line which pops up whenever they pause the mouse pointer on the field.

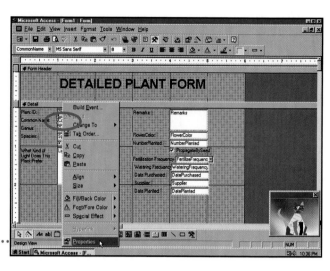

1 Select the **CommonName** field by clicking it, and then right-click the mouse to display the shortcut menu. Select **Properties**.

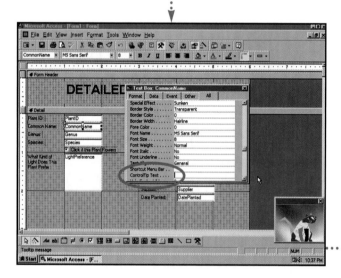

2 The Properties sheet is displayed. Move down the properties sheet list until you come to the **ControlTip Text** property.

3 Enter **Type the Plant's common name here**. You'll see the text scroll out of the text box, but the text is still there. You can enter a maximum of 256 characters for the tip text. Click the **View** button on the toolbar.

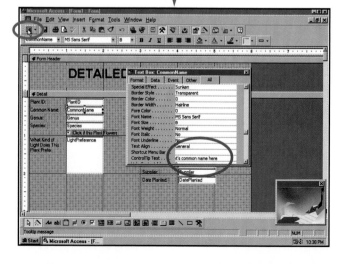

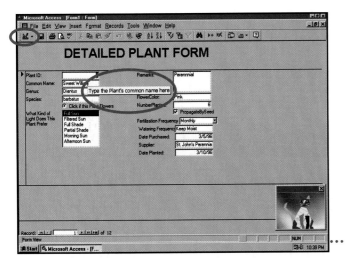

4 You will see your form in Form View, as it would appear if you were to use it now. Place the mouse pointer on the **CommonName** field box. See how the tip is displayed after you pause the pointer on the field. Click the **View** button again to return to the Design view window.

5 Click the Close (**X**) button on the Properties sheet to close it. ■

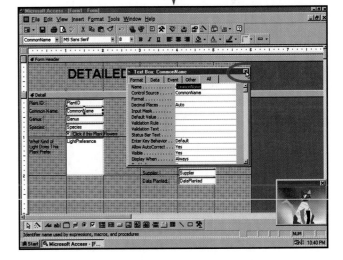

TASK

48

Saving Your New Form

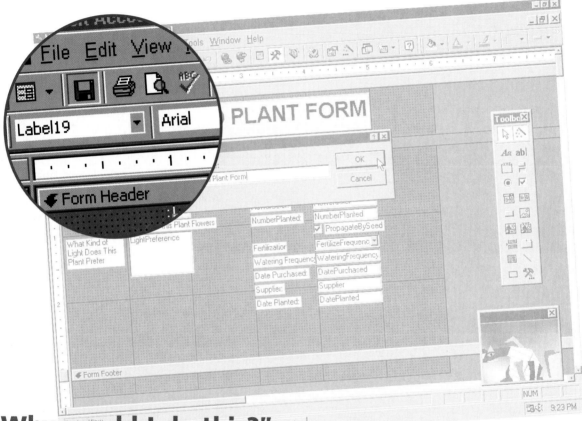

"Why would I do this?"

Once you have completed your form you must save it or you will loose all of your work. Access doesn't automatically save a Design view form as it does with a form created with the Form Wizard. Once you have saved a form, it will be placed on the Forms list and will be available for later use.

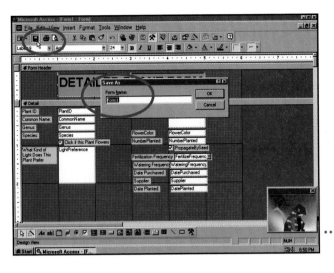

1 Click the **Save** button on the toolbar. The Save As dialog box appears.

Missing Link

You can also select **File**, **Save** from the menu, or use the keyboard combination **Ctrl+S** to save a form or any other database object. If the form has been saved previously, you will not get this dialog box.

2 Type **Detailed Plant Form** into the Form Name text box. This is the name that Access will use to display your form on the Forms list. You can change the name later.

Puzzled?

You can change any object name in the Database window simply by selecting the object, and then clicking the name once (or by using the F2 key). You will then be in edit mode and you can rename the object.

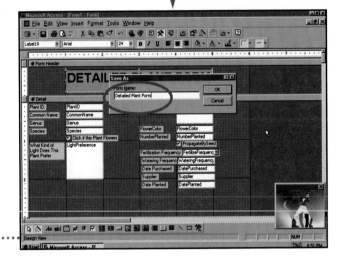

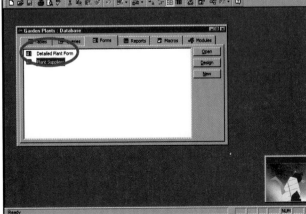

3 Click the **OK** button and then the **Close** (**X**) button on the form window. You now will see your new form displayed in the Forms list on the Database window. ■

Missing Link

Remember, if a form doesn't meet your needs, you can delete it and create another form; or you can simply redesign the form in the Design view window.

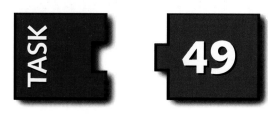

TASK 49

Opening a Form

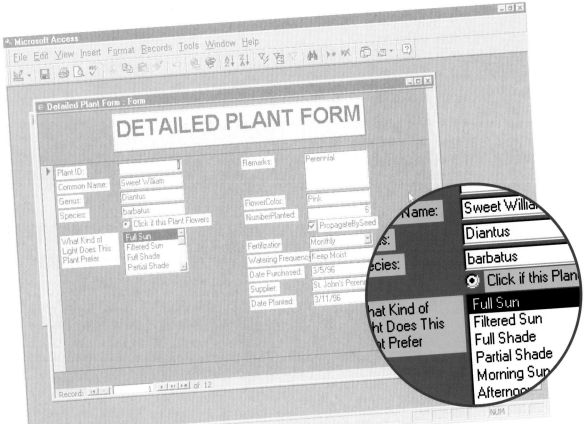

"Why would I do this?"

Just like the table on which a form is based, you must open the form before you can do any real work with it. Once you open the form, you can enter or edit information in the table on which the form is based. Remember, the form is simply another way to view the information contained in the table.

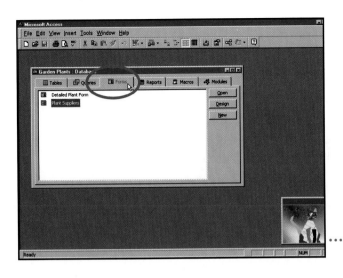

1 Click the **Forms** tab on the Database window to display the list of forms which is now available.

2 Click on the form's name or icon that you want to open. In this example, choose the **Detailed Plant Form**. Click the **Open** button to open the form.

> **Puzzled?**
>
> You can also open a form by double-clicking it.

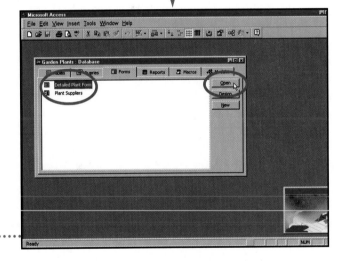

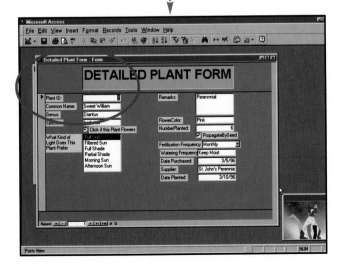

3 The selected form now appears on-screen. If the form window is too small to display the form, you can click the **Maximize** button so that the form appears in the largest window possible. This will help prevent you from unnecessary scrolling to view the form. ■

Entering and Editing Information with a Form

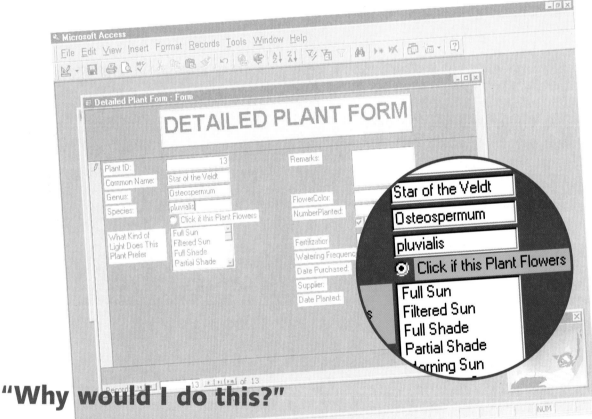

"Why would I do this?"

For most users, the form is the most familiar method of entering or editing information. Everyone is comfortable using a form, and by creating a form which is similar to the paper form you are replacing, you will eliminate mistakes.

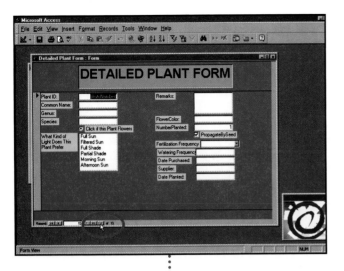

1 Before you can enter new information into a table, you must get to the next new record line. Click the **New Record** button.

Puzzled?

If you load wallpapers when you load Windows 95, your Desktop background may look different than what you see in the figures in this task.

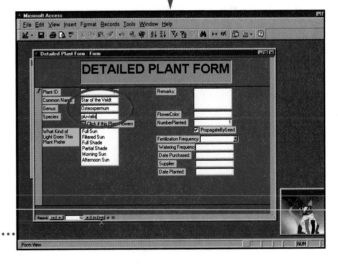

2 Press the **Tab** key to move to the first editable field, **Common Name**, and type **Star of the Veldt**. Press the **Tab** key again to move to the next field. Type **Osteospermum** in the Genus field, and **pluvialis** in the Species field. Be sure to press the **Tab** key to move from field to field.

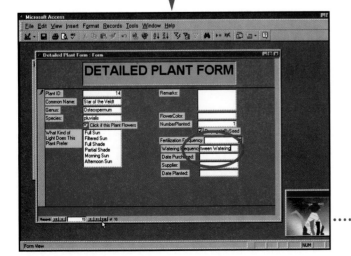

3 Press **Tab** again. The cursor jumps to the **Watering Frequency** field. Type **Dry Out Between Watering**. Access captures everything you type, even if you can't see it in the field. Press **Tab** again.

Puzzled?

If you delete a field, and then place it on your form, the Tab Index changes. This accounts for the cursor simply not moving smoothly down the form in sequence.

4 Type **5/15/96** in the **Date Purchased** field. Be sure to press the **Tab** key to move to each field. Type **St. John's Perennials** in **Place Purchased**; **5/16/96** in **Date Planted**. Press **Tab** twice and type **White** in the **FlowerColor** field; **6** in **NumberPlanted**. Press **Tab** again and press the **Spacebar** to place a check mark in the **PropagateBySeed** check box, indicating that this plant can be grown from seed. Press **Tab** again.

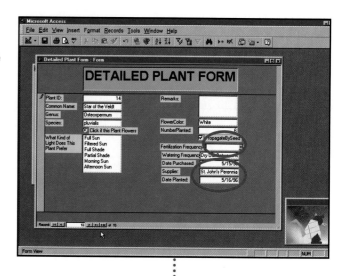

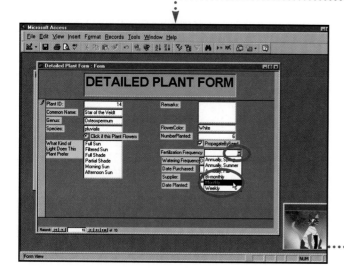

5 The cursor should be in the **Fertilization Frequency** field. Click the arrow button on this combo box field to display the list of options and select **Monthly** from the list. Press the **Tab** key.

6 The cursor should be in the **Light Preference** list box field. Choose the option **Full Sun**. Press the **Tab** key.

Missing Link

To choose a different option in the list box, press the up- or down-arrow keys on your keyboard, or use the scroll bar. The option that is highlighted when you exit the field is the selection which Access enters into the corresponding field in the Plants table.

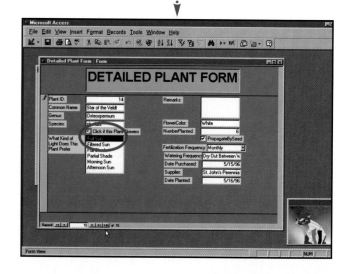

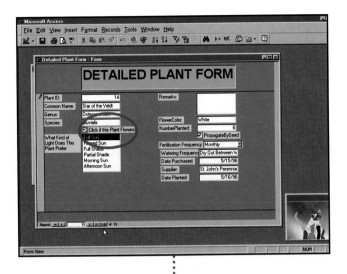

7 The cursor should be at the **Click if this Plant Flowers** option. Press the **Spacebar** to indicate that this plant does produce flowers.

8 Click the **Save** button on the toolbar to save your new record. The record is also automatically saved when you go to a new record. ■

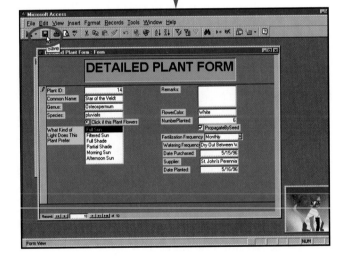

Puzzled?

You can also click the mouse on the option button to select it. When a black dot appears in the circle, it has been selected.

Changing the Field Order

"Why would I do this?"

The order that the cursor moves from field to field on your form as you press the Tab key (or Enter key) is called the Tab Index of the fields. In order for the form to work well for you, the cursor should move from one field to the next, in the order that you expect it to.

The Tab Index order is determined solely on how you placed the fields on your form. For example, in the Detailed Plant Form, you placed all of the fields, and then deleted several and replaced them with other types of controls. When you deleted the fields, they were removed from the Tab Index order for the form, and all of the fields placed after them were moved up in the order. When you placed the new field object, it was placed at the end of the Tab Index

order. So when you tabbed from field to field in the Detailed Plant form in the previous task, the cursor did not land on each field in sequential order.

When you move a field on the form, its Tab Index order doesn't change, even if you place it as the last field on the form. Now, you can always delete all of the fields on your form and then replace them, in both the correct order and position so that your user will move through the form naturally, or you can just change the Tab Index order. You may want to make a list of the fields on your form, and number them in the sequential order that you want them to be accessed when your user presses the Tab key.

1 Click the **View** button to switch the Detailed Plant Form into the Design view window. Select the **Plant ID** field on your form and click the **Properties** button on the toolbar.

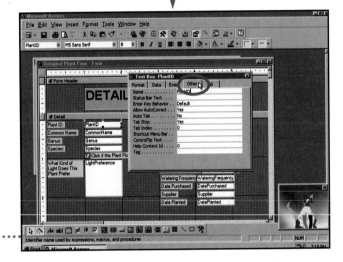

2 The Properties sheet is displayed for this field. Click the **Other** tab on the properties sheet.

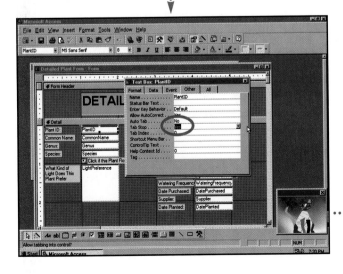

3 This limits the display to only a few properties, including Tab Index and Tab Stop properties. Move the cursor down to the **Tab Stop** text box.

179

4 Change this option from Yes to **No**. The Tab Stop property determines whether the cursor passes through this field or not. When set to Yes, the cursor moves to the field when you press the Tab key.

> ### Puzzled?
>
> The Plant ID is an AutoNumber data type, which you can't change. Setting this property to No causes Access to bypass the field when you press the Tab key. In an editable field, you can use the mouse to move into the field.

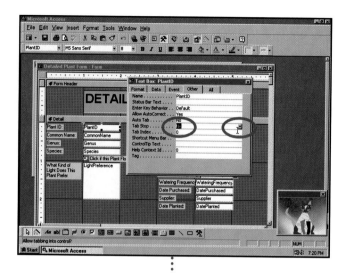

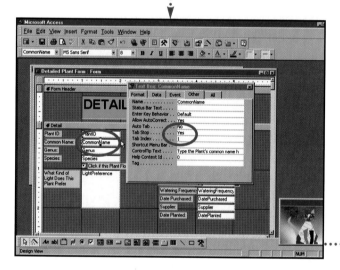

5 After you set the Tab Stop property to No, you don't need to worry about the Tab Index setting. The first field placed on the form is always Tab Index number 0. Use the mouse pointer to select the **CommonName** field on the Design view grid. The Tab Stop is set to Yes, and the Tab Index is set to 1; these don't require changes.

6 Continue to select each field object in the order that you want to select the fields when the Tab key is pressed. Check the Tab Index number for each field to make sure that the number is one larger than the previous field. Access automatically adjusts all of the remaining field's Tab Index numbers. Change the option button Plant Flowers from 14 to **4**.

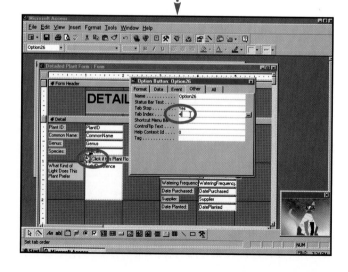

7 Change the **LightPreference** field's Tab Index from 14 to **5**.

Puzzled?

Access doesn't enable you to create duplicate Tab Index numbers. For example, if you change Tab Index 10 to 3, then the field that once had Tab Index 3 would become 4, and so on back to 9, which would become 10.

8 Change the Tab Index properties as indicated: Remarks, **6**; FlowerColor, **7**; NumberPlanted, **8**; PropagateBySeed, **9**; and FertilizeFrequency, **10**. The remaining fields shouldn't need to be changed because Access will have automatically made the necessary adjustments.

Puzzled?

Drag the property sheet from one side of the form to the other if it covers the field objects that you need to select.

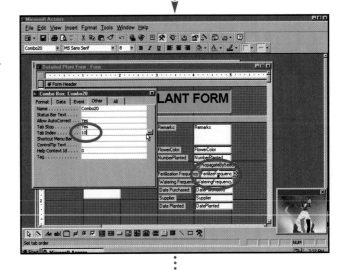

9 Click the **View** button again and test the new Tab Index order. The form opens with the first record and the cursor is in the Common Name field instead of the Plant ID field. Press the **Tab** key to move through each field, checking the Tab Index. If all is OK, then click the **Save** button to save your changes, otherwise, go back to Design view and make additional adjustments. ■

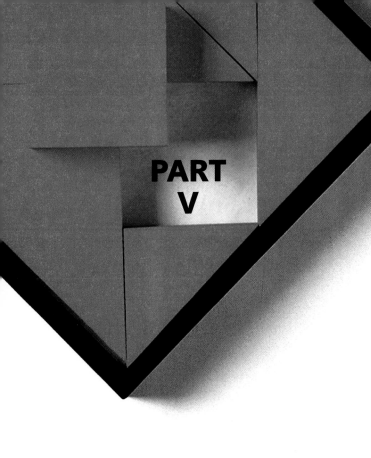

PART V

Getting Information from a Database

52 Creating a Select Query

53 Using the Crosstab Query

54 Selecting Records with Wild Cards

55 Selecting Records with an "OR" Criterion

56 Selecting Records with More than One Criterion

57 Using Arithmetic Operators

▲ ● ■ ● ■ ● ■ ● ▲ ●

ONE OF THE MOST POWERFUL FEATURES included with Access is the ability to ask questions about the information that has been collected. A question is built in the form of an example and is called a *query*. Unlike a simple card file where you can look up one record at a time—usually in alphabetical order, Access can respond to a query by finding all records that meet certain *criteria*. Criteria are simply restrictions that Access uses to select the information which will be displayed in the *results set*. The results set is the group of records which meets the criteria you have entered.

There are several different types of queries which you can create; each of which produces a different result. The most commonly used are:

- **Select Query** This type of query enables you to specify various criteria for Access to use in selecting records. The selected records are displayed as a results set in a Datasheet view of the query, or can be used in a report or form.

- **Crosstab Query** This type of query is often used to graph information from one or more tables. You create a Crosstab query to display trends and generate summaries of information about groups of records. There is a Crosstab Wizard that you use to help create this type of query. It is often used to compare one aspect of your records to another.

- **Action Query** This type of query is used to add information to, or edit information in, a group of records in either an existing table or a new table. For example, you can use an action query to update the prices of items that you sell, or to delete all customers who have not purchased products in the last two years.

Criteria can include more than one field or table. For example, you can create a query which finds and displays all customers who live in the United States and who bought more than $500 worth of merchandise in the past year on a single order.

Some of the tasks for which you can design a query are the following:

- Showing records that meet specified criteria (Select Query)

- Displaying selected data from a table, sorted in a specific order (Select Query)

- Updating specific fields in selected records with new information (Update Query)

- Displaying selected records from several tables at once (Select Query)

- Adding information from one table to another (Update Query)

- Deleting selected information or records from a table (Delete Query)

Once you create a query, you can use the query as the basis for a form or report. You can build a query that uses information from several tables. For example, you can combine information from a Sales table and a Customer table to find out who your best customers are based on amount of sales. Basing a report on a query ensures that the report has the most up-to-date information. You can easily build a query that selects all customers who have past-due invoices. Then use the results set to create a report that lists these customers, their phone numbers, the invoices that are past due, and displays a subtotal for each customer.

When you begin to build queries, write them down in either a question or statement form. Putting a question on paper will help you to focus on the information which you need. It will also help you to revise a query which isn't displaying the information you are looking for. Be as specific as possible in building your query statement and refine it if necessary. The more specific you are when you write your question, the easier it is to build the actual query.

Creating a Select Query

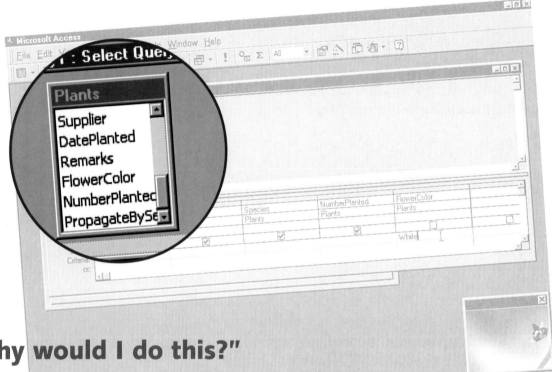

"Why would I do this?"

The most common query that you will use is probably the select query. With this query you can choose records that meet the criteria you specify, and then display the results set in a datasheet.

For example, you can build a query for the statement, "Display all records for plants that have white flowers, and include only the Common Name, Genus, Species, and Number Planted." This simple query statement causes

Access to look through your Plants table searching first for all of the records which have the color "white" in the FlowerColor field. If a plant meets this criteria, then it is included in the results set. This results set will also include only the fields you specified (Common Name, Genus, Species, and Number Planted), rather than displaying all of the fields in the table.

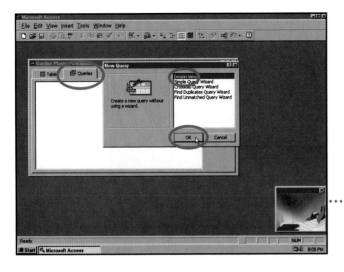

1 Click the **Queries** tab button on the Database window. You'll see a blank Query list since you haven't yet created any queries. Click the **New** button on the Database window. Access displays the New Query dialog box. Select the **Design View** option, and then click the **OK** button.

2 The Show Table dialog box is displayed on top of the Select Query window. Be sure that the **Tables** tab is selected, and choose the **Plants** table from the list. Click the **Add** button to place the selected table onto the query Design view grid.

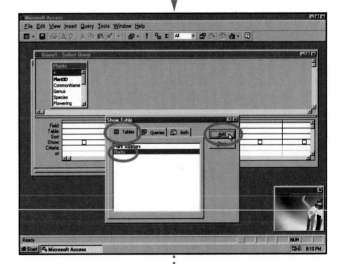

Missing Link

If you plan to base the query on the results of another query, click the **Queries** tab button to display a list of available queries. if you want to use both queries and tables, click the **Both** tab button.

3 Since the query in our example is based on the Plants table only, click the **Close** button to remove the Show Table dialog box.

Missing Link

Select all the tables that would be used in the query before clicking Close (**X**).

4 From the Plants list box, double-click the field **CommonName**. Access immediately places that field in the first column of the query grid.

Missing Link

If you double-click the asterisk to include all fields, Access will add a single column, which you can't use to sort.

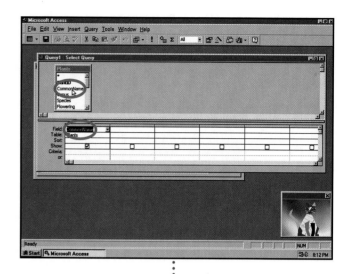

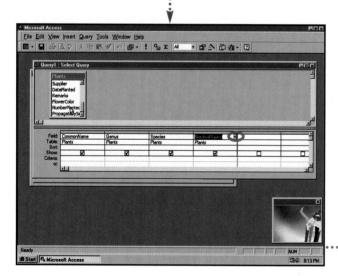

5 Click the mouse pointer in the Field row of the second column of the grid and click the arrow button displayed. From the drop-down list of field names which appears, choose **Genus** as the second field for this query. Add the **Species** and **NumberPlanted** as the third and fourth columns using either method from step 4 or 5.

6 Finally, place the **FlowerColor** field onto the query grid.

Puzzled?

If you can't see a selected field on the query grid, use the horizontal scroll bar at the bottom of the window to see if it is simply too far to the right to be seen. You can resize the columns by double-clicking the right edge of any column selector button directly above the Field cell. The column automatically adjusts to accurately fit the information in it.

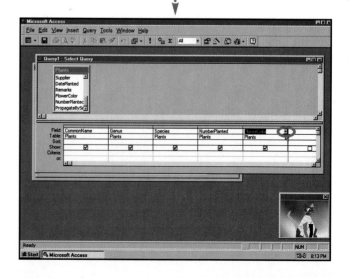

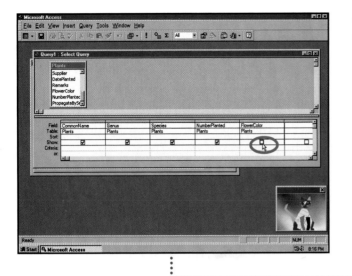

7 Click the check box in the row labeled **Show** in the FlowerColor column. This removes the check mark, indicating that this field will not be displayed in the results set. This allows you to use a column for criteria selection or sorting, without displaying it.

> **Missing Link**
>
> You can always click the Show check box again, so that the field will appear in the results set.

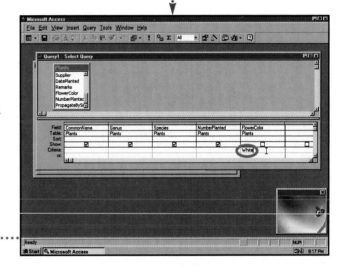

8 Press the down arrow key, moving the cursor to the Criteria row of the FlowerColor column, and type **White**. This is the actual criterion that any selected record must meet: it must have white—and only white—flowers.

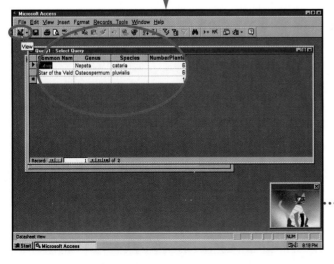

9 Click either the **View** or **Run** button on the toolbar to display the results set for this query. After you've viewed the results of the query, click the Close (**X**) button.

> **Missing Link**
>
> In an Action query, the **View** button shows you the results set while the **Run** button actually performs the query.

10 The Office Assistant displays a balloon asking you if you want to save this query; click the **Yes** button.

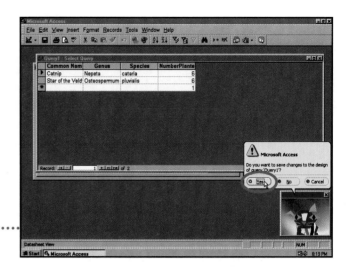

11 In the Save As dialog box type **Select Plants By Flower Color** in the text box, and then click the **OK** button.

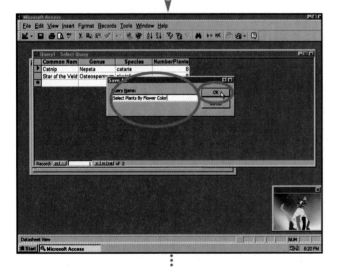

> ### Puzzled?
>
> If the query didn't perform as you expected, simply click the **View** button again to return to the Design view window. Make any necessary adjustments and then view the new results set.

12 The new query is added to the Queries list in the Database window. You can easily reuse this query to choose plants with colors other than white, by simply changing the color criteria from White to any other color. ■

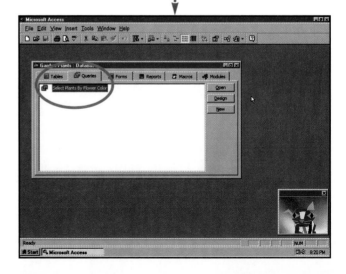

Using the Crosstab Query

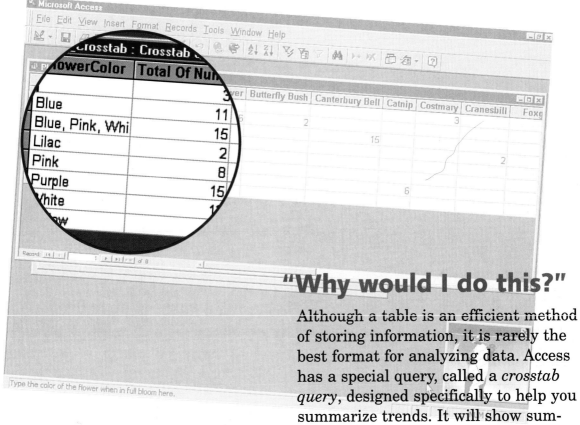

"Why would I do this?"

Although a table is an efficient method of storing information, it is rarely the best format for analyzing data. Access has a special query, called a *crosstab query*, designed specifically to help you summarize trends. It will show summary values by comparing the data from one field with the data contained in other fields.

In this task, using the Plants table, you will create a crosstab query to answer the query statement, "How many plants of each color do I have planted?" This statement compares the number of plants you have according to their color.

1 Open the Query list by clicking the **Queries** tab button, and then click the **New** button. Select the **Crosstab Query Wizard** from the New Query dialog box, and click **OK**.

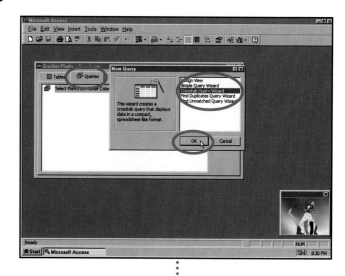

Missing Link

Remember, you can also begin a new query by either pressing **Ctrl+N**, or selecting **Insert**, **Query** from the menu, or selecting Query from the New Object button's list.

2 The first Crosstab Query Wizard dialog box appears. Like building a query from scratch, Access selects the Tables option by default. Select the **Plants** table from the list and click the **Next >** button.

Missing Link

You can also double-click the Crosstab Query Wizard option in the New Query dialog box to select it and launch the wizard.

3 Choose the field you want to use as the comparison field, in this case **FlowerColor**, by selecting it and clicking the **>** button. This field moves to the Selected Fields list. Click the **Next >** button.

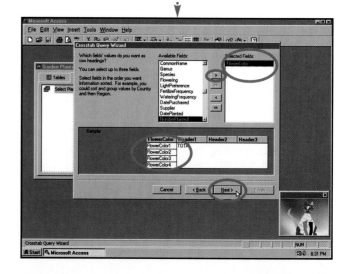

Puzzled?

You can choose a maximum of three fields for your row headers, enabling you to sort and group fields together.

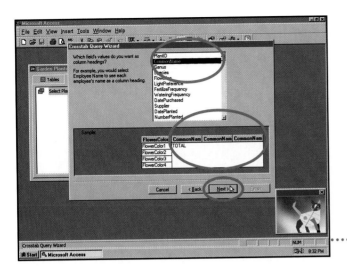

4 Choose the field which acts as the column heading by selecting the field **CommonName**. Click the **Next >** button.

5 Choose the field that will be used to compare the previously selected fields to each other. In this example, you're comparing numbers of plants by color to name, so select the **NumberPlanted** field. Now choose the type of summary calculation you want to display; here you want the **Sum** function. Be sure that the check box **Yes, include row sums** is selected. Click the **Next >** button.

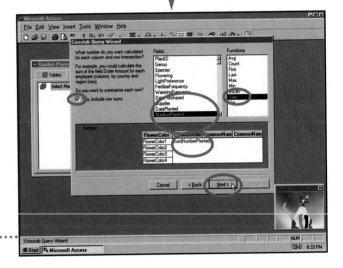

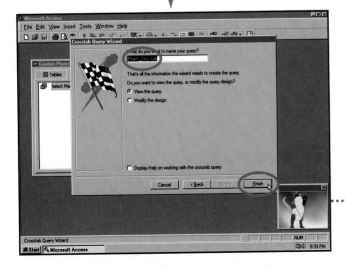

6 Plants Crosstab is fine as the title of this query. You can easily override it by typing a new name. Click the **Finish** button.

7 The results set is now displayed in a datasheet. Each of the various colors of flowers is listed in the leftmost column, while the plant common names are listed as column heads. A summary column, giving you the total number of plants in each color, is displayed as the second column. The first row has no flower color listed. If you scroll through the datasheet you'll find that one plant, Costmary, has no color listed; either you didn't enter a color, or the plant doesn't flower.

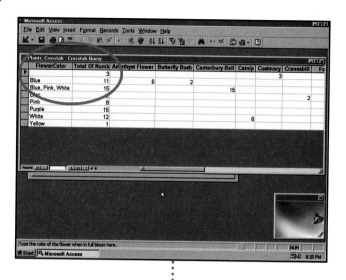

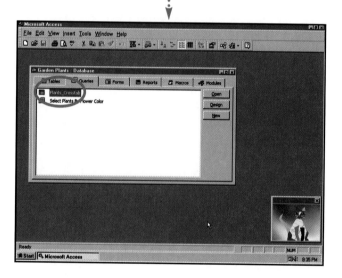

8 Click the Close (**X**) button. It will now appear on your Queries list. The query was automatically saved with the wizard. ■

Puzzled?

The field(s) you select for row headings do not appear as choices for column headings. This happens because you can't create a comparison of a thing to itself.

Selecting Records with Wild Cards

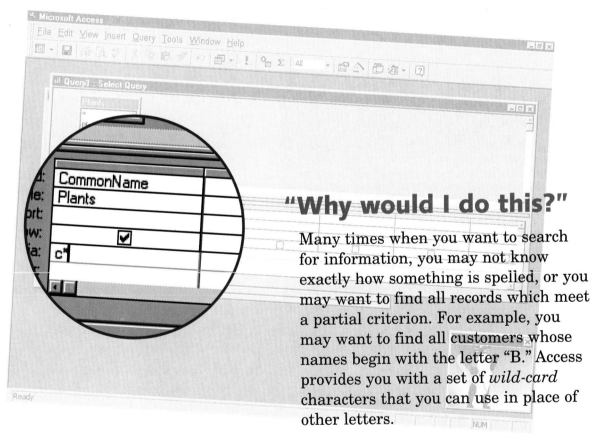

"Why would I do this?"

Many times when you want to search for information, you may not know exactly how something is spelled, or you may want to find all records which meet a partial criterion. For example, you may want to find all customers whose names begin with the letter "B." Access provides you with a set of *wild-card* characters that you can use in place of other letters.

The most common wildcard characters are the asterisk (*) and the question mark (?). An asterisk represents any number of any character, while the question mark represents any single character.

1 Open the **Queries** list and select the **New** button. Choose **Design View** from the list and click the **OK** button.

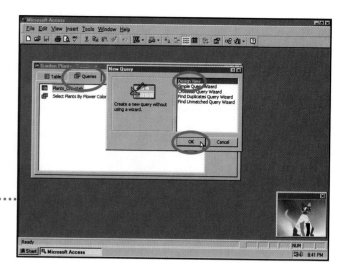

2 In the Show Table dialog box, select the **Plants** table from the list and click the **Add** button. The Plants field list appears in the Select Query window. Click the **Close** button on the Show Table dialog box.

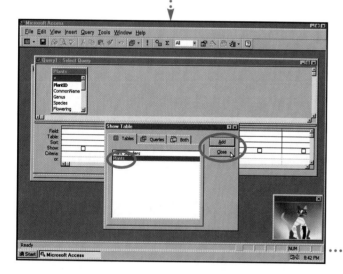

3 Double-click the field **CommonName** to add it to the query grid. Move the cursor down to the Criteria row in the same column.

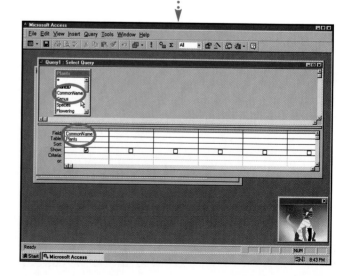

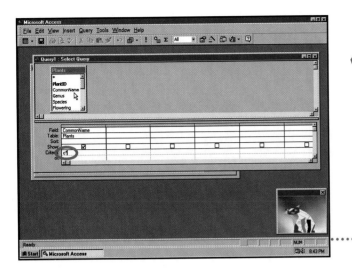

4 Type **c*** to tell Access to search for all plants with a common name that begins with the letter "C" and display them in the results set. Press an arrow key, or click the mouse pointer in another cell of the grid. Notice that Access changes the criterion to read Like "c*". Click the **View** button on the toolbar.

5 Access displays the results set in a datasheet. Click the Close (**X**) button.

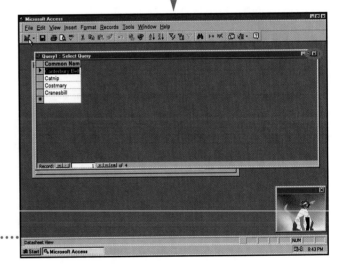

Puzzled?

If you see a datasheet with no records, this means that no records were found that met your criteria. Look at your query statement again. If it's correct, you may want to manually check for records in the table that do meet your criteria, to ensure that they do exist.

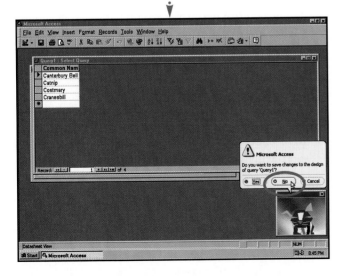

6 When the Office Assistant prompts you to save the new query select the **No** button. ■

197

TASK **55**

Selecting Records with an "OR" Criterion

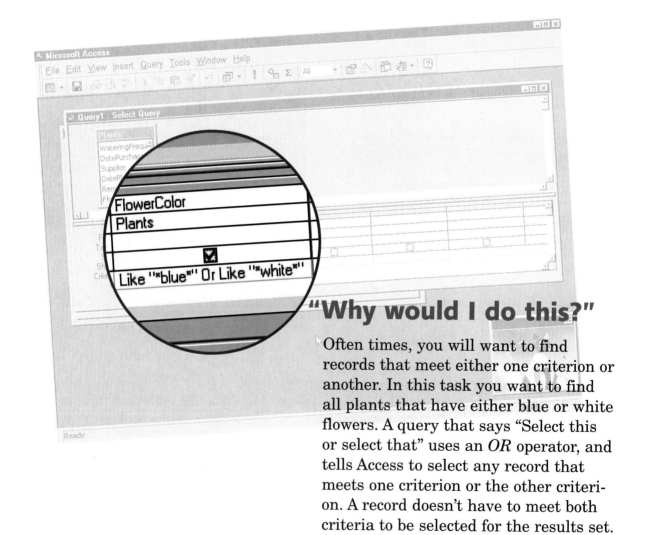

"Why would I do this?"

Often times, you will want to find records that meet either one criterion or another. In this task you want to find all plants that have either blue or white flowers. A query that says "Select this or select that" uses an *OR* operator, and tells Access to select any record that meets one criterion or the other criterion. A record doesn't have to meet both criteria to be selected for the results set.

OR criteria can be setup across multiple fields. For example, a query which asks "Select customers from the state of NY, or from the city of Los Angeles" is a multiple field OR criterion.

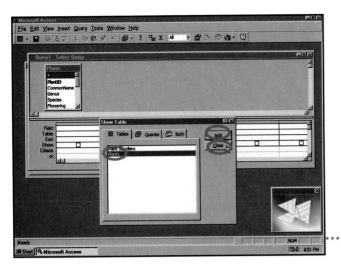

1 Open the **Queries** list and select the **New** button. Choose **Design View** from the list and click **OK**. Double-click the **Plants** table for this query and then **Close** the Show Table dialog box.

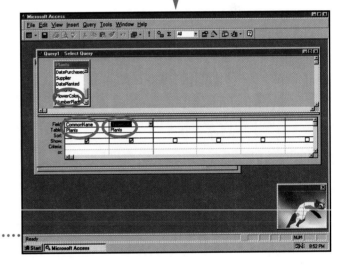

2 Select the field **CommonName** from the list by double-clicking it. It is displayed in the grid on the bottom half of the Query screen. Locate **FlowerColor** in the field list (use the scroll bar) and double-click it to add it to the grid.

3 In the Criteria row of the FlowerColor column, type `"*blue*" Or "*white*"` and then press the up arrow key.

Missing Link

Asterisks ensure that plants with multiple flower colors are included. Access adds the word "Like" with wild-card characters.

199

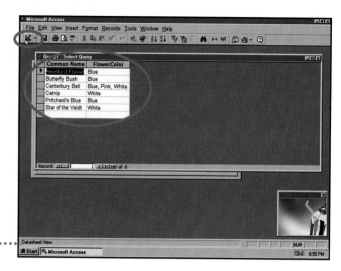

4 Click the **View** button.

> **Puzzled?**
>
> An "OR" criterion can be broken into two parts and placed in separate criteria rows. Notice that the row below the Criteria row is labeled "or." You could type the first criteria "*blue*" in the Criteria row, and then type the second criteria "*white*" into the second row.

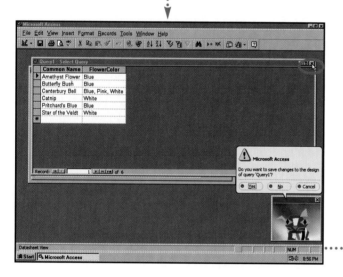

5 The results set appears in datasheet form for this query. Click the Close (**X**) button on the Datasheet window.

6 Click the **Yes** button on the Office Assistant's balloon asking if you want to save this query. Save this query using the name **Select Multiple Flower Colors** in the Save As dialog box and then click the **OK** button. Access has added the new query to the Queries list. ■

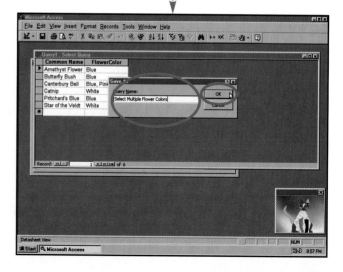

Selecting Records with More than One Criterion

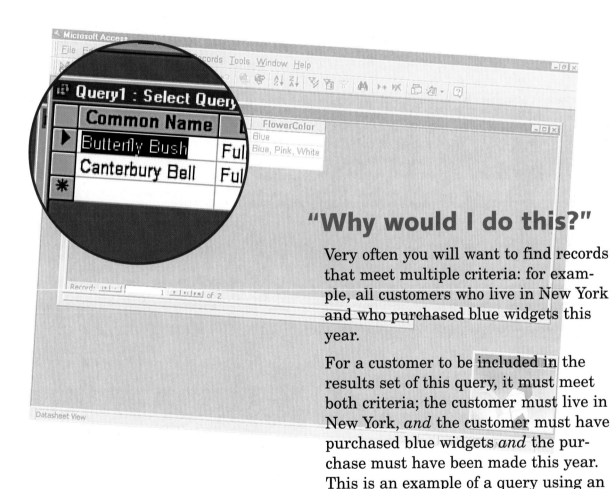

"Why would I do this?"

Very often you will want to find records that meet multiple criteria: for example, all customers who live in New York and who purchased blue widgets this year.

For a customer to be included in the results set of this query, it must meet both criteria; the customer must live in New York, *and* the customer must have purchased blue widgets *and* the purchase must have been made this year. This is an example of a query using an AND operator. In this task, you will use an AND operator criterion to find all plants with blue flowers AND that require full sunlighting conditions.

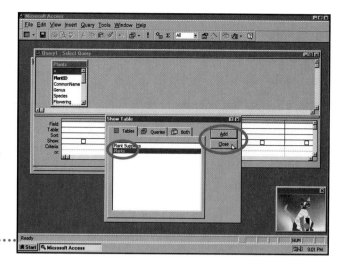

1 Open the **Queries** list and select the **New** button. Choose **Design View** and click the **OK** button. Double-click the **Plants** table, adding it to the query Design view window, and then close the Show Table dialog box.

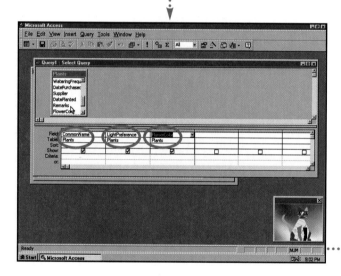

2 Add these fields (locate each field in the Plants list and double-click) to the query grid: **CommonName**, **LightPreference**, and **FlowerColor**.

3 Move the cursor to the Criteria row of the LightPreference column and type **"*full sun*"** as your entry. Move the cursor to the Criteria row for the FlowerColor column and type **"*blue*"** in the column, then click in another cell.

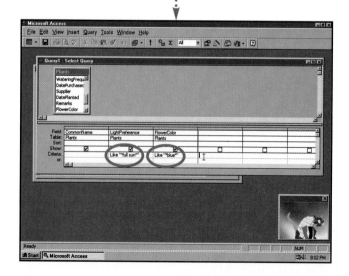

Puzzled?

You must enter the criteria in the same row for them to be considered an AND operator. Criteria entered in separate rows are considered by Access to be OR criteria.

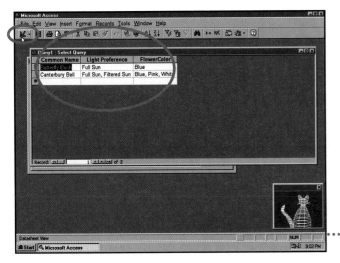

4 Click the **View** button to see the results set for this query. Two records meet these criteria; notice how the second record would've been excluded without the wild cards in the color criteria.

5 Click the Close (**X**) button. Don't save the query when prompted by the Office Assistant. ■

Missing Link

If your results set includes records that don't meet both criteria you entered, check the query grid again. Be sure that you didn't add the criteria on different rows and accidentally create an "OR" query instead.

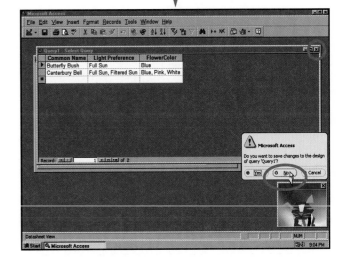

TASK **57**

Using Arithmetic Operators

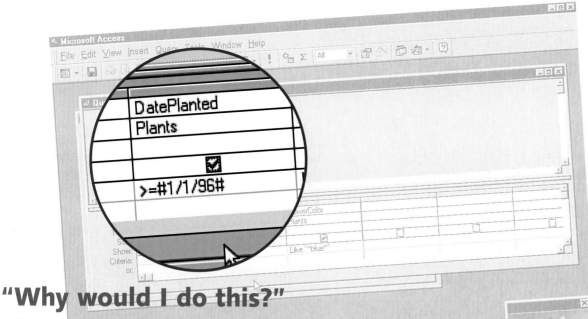

"Why would I do this?"

Several of the arithmetic operators can be used with both text or numeric data types. The most commonly used arithmetic operators include = (equal), + (plus), < (less than), > (greater than), <= (less than or equal to), and >= (greater than or equal to). These operators can be used with both text and numeric data. In contrast, the following arithmetic operators are most often used only with numeric information: - (minus), * (multiply), / (divide).

For example, you can use an arithmetic operator in a query to display records for customers whose last names begin

with the letter "F" up to and including "M" like this: (>="F" AND <="M"). Alternatively, you can use the multiply operators to multiply the values in one field by the values contained in another and display the results in a new column. You can create this expression by entering it into the Field row of a blank column in the query grid like this: (ExtendedPrice:[UnitPrice]*[Quantity]) This is often how an extended price is displayed in a form or report.

In this task, you'll create a query which displays all plants with blue flowers that were planted on or after January 1, 1996.

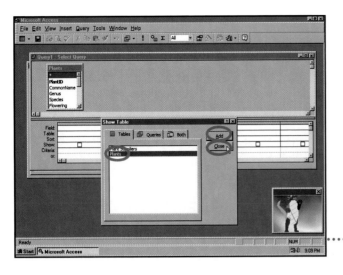

1 Open the New Query dialog box, and select **Design View** from the list, and click the **OK** button. Select the **Plants** table for this query and then close the Show Table dialog box.

2 From the Plants field list select **CommonName**, **DatePlanted**, and **FlowerColor**, placing each onto the query grid.

Puzzled?

Since this query requires the answer to meet both criteria, the query uses an AND operator. Be sure you enter both criteria on the same row.

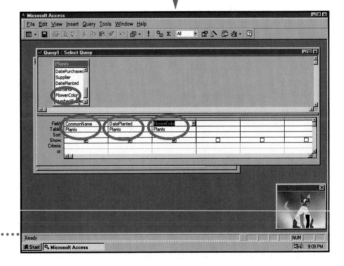

3 The first part of the query statement is "display all plants that have blue flowers." Move the cursor to the Criteria row in the FlowerColor column and type **"*blue*"** as the entry. Access changes the criteria to read Like "*blue*" once you move the cursor from the cell.

4 Move the cursor to the Criteria row in the DatePlanted column. Type **>=1/1/96** into the criteria cell and then press the up arrow key. Notice how Access changes this entry to read >=#1/1/96# in the Criteria row. In a query, the two **#** symbols indicate that the numbers between them are a date value.

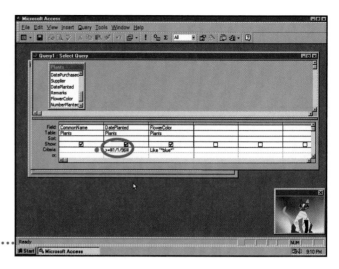

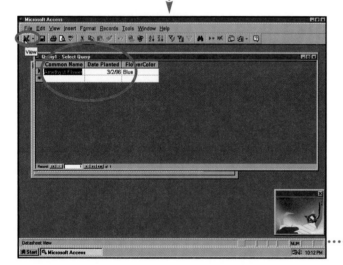

5 Click the **View** button to see the results set for this query.

6 Close the datasheet without saving it when prompted by the Office Assistant. You don't have to return to the Query Design view in order to close the query. ■

Missing Link

If your query displays records that meet one or the other criterion, you may have built an "OR" query by entering the criteria on separate lines. Make sure that the criteria statements are on the same line to create an "AND" query.

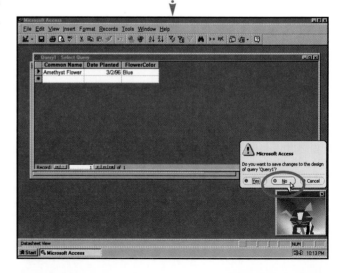

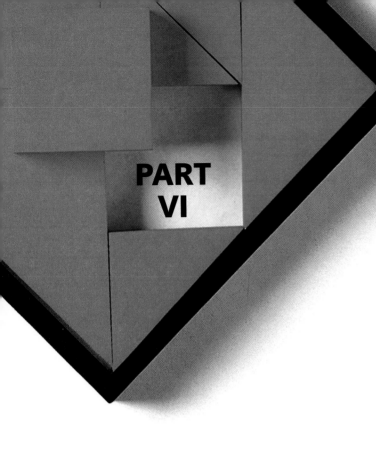

PART VI

Creating and Using Reports

58 Building a Report with a Wizard

59 Creating a Report in Design View

60 Using Groups and Sorting

61 Using Labels in a Report

62 Printing a Report

WHILE YOU CAN PRINT COPIES OF YOUR TABLES, forms, and the results set of a query, you have greater control over your information's format when it is printed as a report. In many ways, building a report is similar to designing a form: You can choose how to group records with a report, select fields to be included, and decide on the placement of those fields within the report layout. Most of the techniques that you learned when designing a form also apply directly to designing a report. You can also create a report that displays subtotals for selected groups of records, or for each page, and then include a final total for the entire report at the end. When you build a report, you can easily add summary information such as totals, subtotals, and percentages, for groups of records, or for the report as a whole.

Often, a report is based on a query instead of a table. This allows you to have a great deal of control over the information that is included in the report. If you simply base the report on a table, then all of the records contained in the table will be included. If you base the report on a query, the query is run before the report is actually printed. This procedure allows you to use the query to select records and combine information from multiple tables.

You can create reports for a variety of purposes, including:

Mailing labels, invoices, product shelf tags, address and phone lists, analysis of sales and purchases, lists of sales contacts, and account-collections letters.

You can create a report by using either a Report Wizard or by building your report from the Design view window. A report created with a Report Wizard can use more than one table. The following is a list of the three Report Wizards and two

AutoReports which you can choose from to help you easily build a report:

- **Report Wizard**   This wizard enables you to create a report with the greatest control. You can choose more than one table or query on which to base the report, and you can select the fields that you want to display. You can also choose to group records by a specific field(s), and you can determine how to sort records within a group. You can print the report in either portrait or landscape mode and you have a choice of six field styles or layouts.

- **Chart Wizard**   This wizard creates a report that displays a chart, or graph of information selected from tables or queries. You have 12 different chart styles to select from, including several versions of pie, bar, line, and area graphs.

- **Label Wizard**   The Label Wizard enables you to print on many standard size labels for either continuous-feed or sheet-feed printers. You can use these labels as mailing labels, product labels, or any other kind of label.

- **AutoReport: Columnar**   This report is very similar in structure to the AutoForm. Each field appears inside a box, with its label displayed to the left.

- **AutoReport: Tabular**   This report displays all field labels at the top of each page of the report with the records below. Each page displays as many records as will fit on the page (this varies according to the types of fields in the selected table or query and the font selected for printing. If all of the fields can't fit across a single page, then Access displays the remaining fields on page two; the next group of records will begin on page three.

Reports can include color and reverse printing (white text on black background). Use these options with discretion. Color and reverse printing work best if you can print the report with a color inkjet or laser printer. Even then, color can cause your report's printing time to be unacceptably long. If you use a dot-matrix printer, limit yourself to simple text and lines or your report may become illegible.

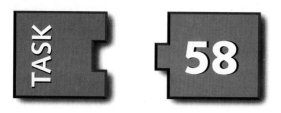

Building a Report
with a Wizard

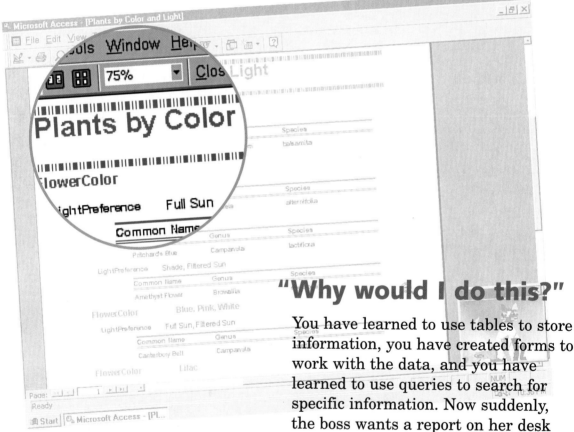

"Why would I do this?"

You have learned to use tables to store information, you have created forms to work with the data, and you have learned to use queries to search for specific information. Now suddenly, the boss wants a report on her desk by quitting time today. What should you do?

By using the Report Wizard, you can quickly create a report that has a polished, professional appearance. You have a choice of several styles for the report layout and how records will be grouped.

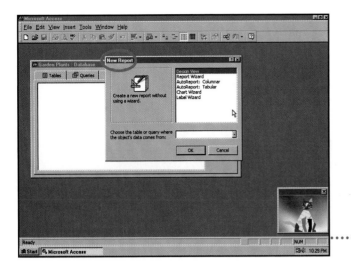

1 Click the **Reports** tab on the Database window. This, like the other lists when first opened, is blank because you have not yet created and saved any reports. Any new reports you create will be added to this list. Click the **New** button.

2 You'll see the New Report dialog box displayed. Select **Report Wizard** from the list box. From the combo box select the **Plants** table. This will be the table on which the report is based. This combo box displays all tables and queries available in the database. Click the **OK** button.

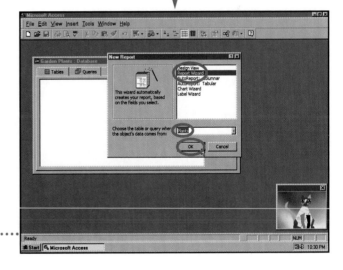

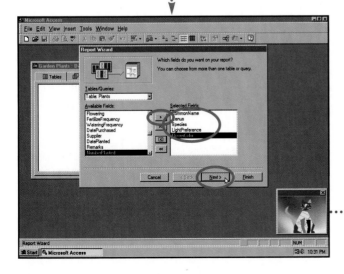

3 Choose the fields to be included on the report by selecting **CommonName**, **Genus**, **Species**, **LightPreference**, and **FlowerColor** fields. Click the **>** button after you select each field. Click the **Next >** button.

4 Choose how you want to group the records by selecting **FlowerColor** and **LightPreference** as the fields to use for grouping. These choices tell Access to group your records first by flower color, and then to subdivide each group by the plant's light preference. Click the **Next >** button.

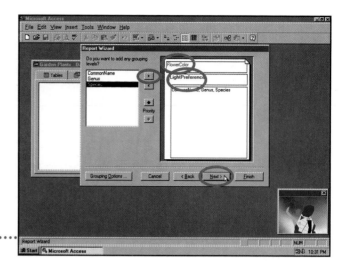

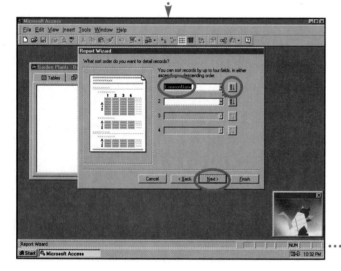

5 Select a field to be used for sorting the records within each detail group, and select the sort order: ascending or descending. In the first combo box select the field **CommonName**. Use the button beside the combo box to choose an ascending sort order, which is the default. Click the **Next >** button.

6 Click each of the Layout option buttons to view the various sample layouts. Select **Outline 1** for this report and then click the **Next >** button.

Puzzled?

If you have more than eight fields selected for the detail records, you may want to choose to print the report in landscape mode. In landscape print mode, Access prints the report across the page, instead of down the page.

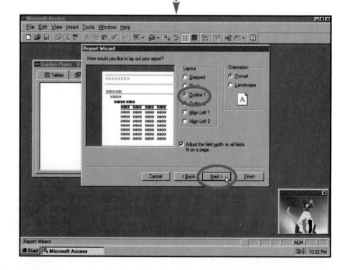

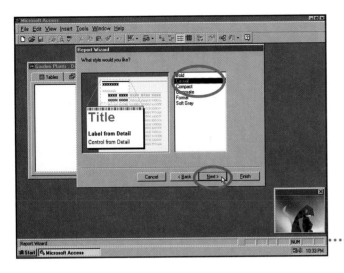

7 Use this dialog box to select a style and font for the report titles. You have six options; again, click through them to see what each looks like. Select the **Casual** option from the list. Click the **Next >** button.

8 Type **Plants by Color and Light** in the text box as the title for this report. If necessary, select the **Preview the report** option button, and Access will open the report in a preview window so that you can view the report on-screen before printing it. Click the **Finish** button to complete the report.

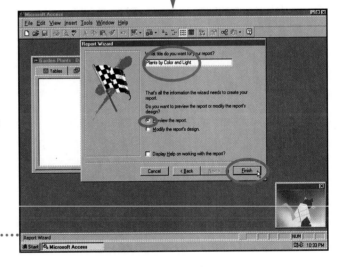

9 Increase the Report Preview window by clicking the **Maximize** button so you can see more of the report. Notice the mouse pointer changes shape to a magnifying glass with a minus sign in the lens. Click the mouse anywhere in the report where it appears as the magnifying glass.

10 You'll see the report shrink so that an entire page fills a screen, and the mouse changes to a magnifying glass with a plus sign in the lens. This view helps you to see the report's page layout—but you can't read much of the text. Click the arrow button on the Zoom combo box in the toolbar and select **75%** from the list.

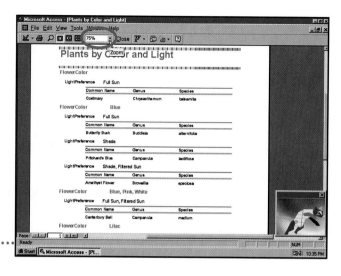

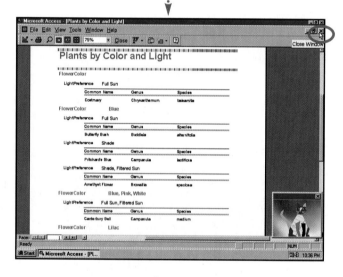

11 You'll see the report increase in size on your screen. Close the report by clicking the Close (**X**) button on the Preview Report window; the report has already been saved by the Report Wizard. ■

Creating a Report in Design View

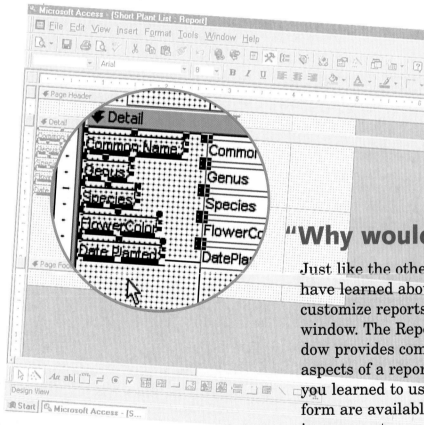

"Why would I do this?"

Just like the other database objects you have learned about, you can create or customize reports in the Design view window. The Report Design view window provides complete control over all aspects of a report. Many of the tools you learned to use when designing a form are available to you when designing a report.

In this task you will learn to create a simple report that will display only specific fields selected from the Plants table. You will be able to either view this report on-screen, or print it.

1 Click the **Reports** tab on the Database window and then click the **New** button. Select **Design View** from the list box on the New Report dialog box, and choose the **Plants** table from the combo box. Click the **OK** button.

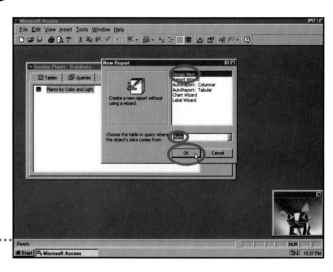

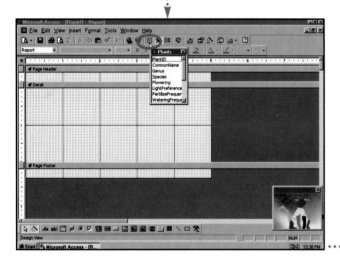

2 The report's Design view window appears. Click the **Maximize** button on the Design view window to give yourself the most room possible. Open the field list by clicking the **Field List** button on the toolbar.

3 Select the field **CommonName**. Now drag the field from the Field List and drop it on the report Detail grid. This is the section of the form that will contain all objects which have to do with the details of the report.

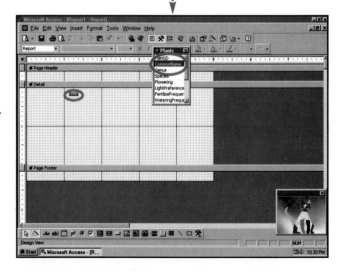

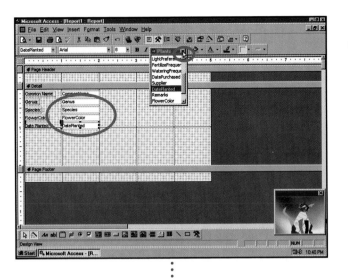

4 Now drag and drop the fields **Genus**, **Species**, **FlowerColor**, and **DatePlanted** onto the detail grid. Close the Field List box by clicking its **Close** (**X**) button.

> **Puzzled?**
>
> To change any of the text attributes within a label box, you must first select the label box. Access then applies any changes to all of the text within the box.

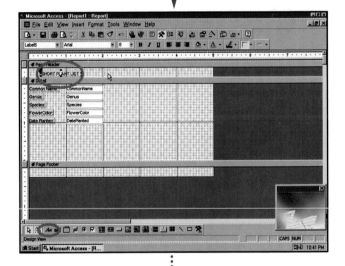

5 Click the **Label** button on the toolbox. Move the label pointer up to the Page Header grid and click once. You'll see a very narrow text box with the insertion point blinking inside of it. Type **SHORT PLANT LIST** and press the **Enter** key to select the label box. Access automatically increases the size of the box to fit your label as you type.

6 Click the arrow on the **Font Size** button and choose **16** as the new font size. Next, click the **Bold** button and then the **Center** button. Increase the size of the label box by dragging the lower right handle toward the bottom of the page header grid and then to the 4-inch grid line.

7 Select all of the attached label boxes for the fields in the report detail area. Click the right mouse button, displaying a short-cut menu. Select **Special Effects** from the menu, and then select the **Shadowed** button. This makes the labels stand out from the field values, making the report easier to read.

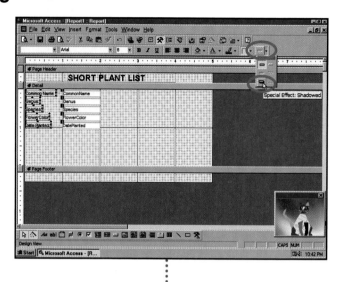

Missing Link

You can select report objects just as you selected form objects. You can use the mouse pointer to drag a box touching each object you want to select.

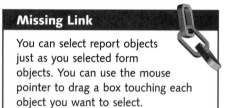

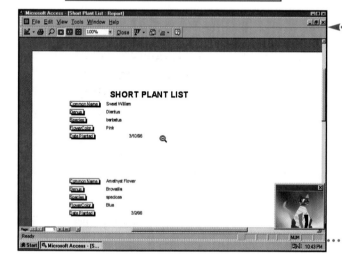

8 Click the **Save** button on the toolbar and type **Short Plant-List** in the Save As dialog box text box. This will be the name for the new report. Finally, click the **OK** button. Click the **View** button to see how your printed report will look.

9 Click the report to view the entire page on-screen. Click the **Close** button on the tool-bar to return to the Design view window. ■

Puzzled?

Notice how the fields in this report are all clustered at the left margin. This should be corrected. We'll do so in the next two tasks.

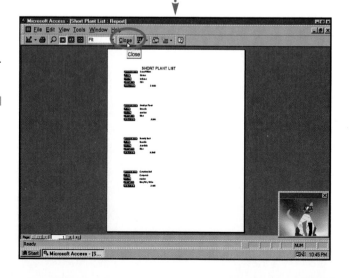

Using Groups and Sorting

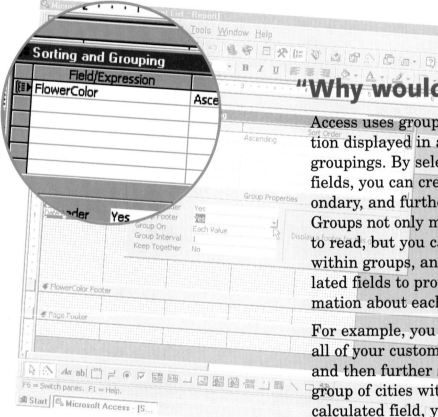

"Why would I do this?"

Access uses groups to divide information displayed in a report by logical groupings. By selecting one or more fields, you can create primary, secondary, and further group subdivisions. Groups not only make your report easier to read, but you can also sort records within groups, and you can use calculated fields to provide summary information about each group.

For example, you can create a report for all of your customers, grouped by state, and then further subdivided into a group of cities within the state. Using a calculated field, you can display the total number of customers by cities and by state. Further, you can sort the customer records in alphabetical order by last name within each city group.

In this task, you will learn to use groups by grouping the records displayed in your report by flower color, and then sorted within this group by the common name.

Task 60: Using Groups and Sorting

1 If the Short Plant list is not already open, select **Short Plant List** from the reports list and click the **Design** button. This opens the selected report in the Report Design view window. Be sure to maximize the window. Click the **Sorting and Grouping** button on the toolbar.

Missing Link

You'll use this report as a starting point. You can save the report again with a new name, giving you two reports slightly different from each other.

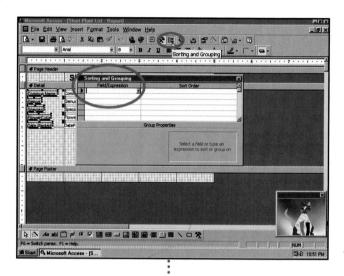

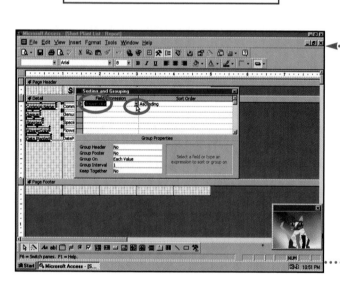

2 In the Sorting and Grouping dialog box that appears, click the arrow button and choose the **FlowerColor** field from the drop-down list.

3 Select the **Yes** option in both the Group Header and Group Footer combo boxes and then click the **Close** (**X**) button.

Puzzled?

To simply sort the report by flower color, leave the Group Header and Footer options on No. Access then uses the selected field to sort your report, but doesn't display a Group Header or Footer.

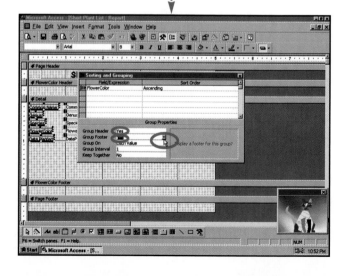

222

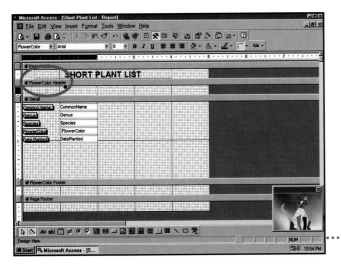

4 You see that Access has added a FlowerColor Header and FlowerColor Footer grid to the report design. Select the field object **FlowerColor** from the report detail grid and drag it up into the FlowerColor Header grid. Be sure to drag from the field object and not the attached label, or else you will only move the label.

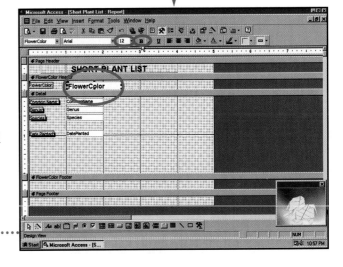

5 Increase the size of the FlowerColor field object by dragging the lower-right handle to the bottom of the header grid, and then to the 2¹/₂-inch grid mark on the horizontal ruler. Now use the **Font Size** tool to increase the font size to **12** and click the **Bold** button.

6 Select the **FlowerColor** label and use the **Special Effects** tool (it's the one on the far right) and select the **Flat** option from the drop-down menu. Next select the **Border Color** tool and click the **Transparent** button on the palette.

223

7 Click the **Line** tool on the toolbox and draw a horizontal line by dragging across the report at the bottom of the FlowerColor header grid. Click the **Border Width** button and select **2-pt Border Width** from the palette. Click the **Sorting and Grouping** button again.

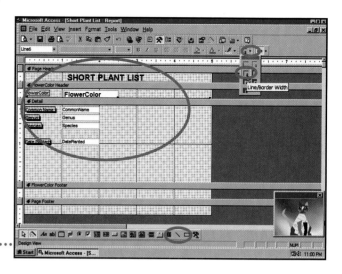

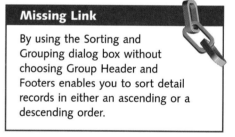

8 In the Sorting and Grouping dialog box, press the down-arrow key once to move to the first blank row. From the combo box select **CommonName** from the list. All other options remain at the default settings.

Missing Link

By using the Sorting and Grouping dialog box without choosing Group Header and Footers enables you to sort detail records in either an ascending or a descending order.

9 Click the **Close (X)** button on the Sorting and Grouping dialog box. ■

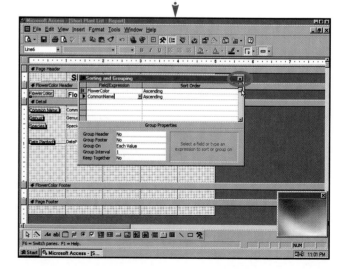

Using Labels in a Report

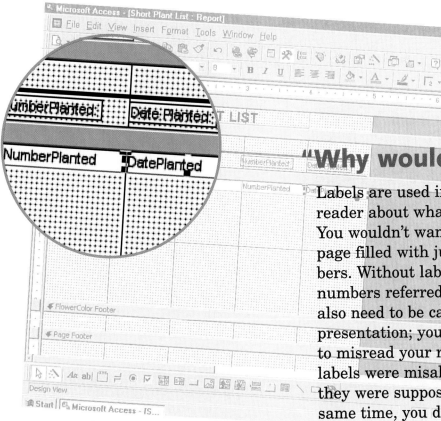

"Why would I do this?"

Labels are used in a report to tell the reader about what they are reading. You wouldn't want to give your boss a page filled with just columns of numbers. Without labels to tell her what the numbers referred to, she'd be lost. You also need to be careful with your labels' presentation; you don't want someone to misread your report because the labels were misaligned with the records they were supposed to go with. At the same time, you don't want to clutter your report with unnecessary labels.

By default, Access will include labels for every field and for every record. Unnecessary labels can easily double the length of a report. By moving labels from the detail grid to the lowest level group header, or to the page header, you can have labels printed once for every group, or once for each page.

1 Click the Field List button and add **NumberPlanted** to the Detail grid. Select each of the field labels in the report's detail grid and move them one-by-one so that they are all in a horizontal line, in this order: Common Name, Genus, Species, Number Planted, Date Planted. Remember, you move the attached label by using the move handle on the label.

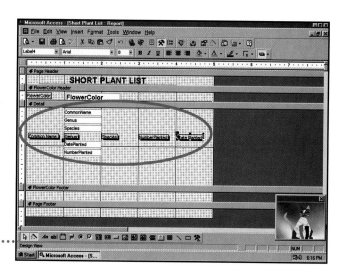

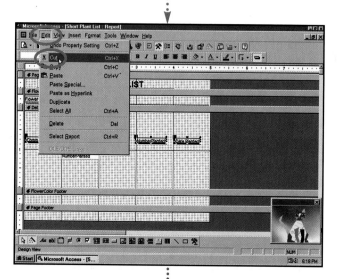

2 Select all five of the field labels and then select **Edit**, **Cut** from the menu. This removes the labels from the Design window and places them on the Windows Clipboard.

Missing Link

Remember, you can use the keyboard combinations **Ctrl+X** to cut selected objects from the window, and **Ctrl+V** to paste the contents of the Windows Clipboard into the window.

3 Move the mouse pointer to the bottom of the FlowerColor header grid and drag the grid down about ½-inch so the header is now ¾-inch in height. Now click the mouse pointer anywhere in the FlowerColor header grid, and then select **Edit**, **Paste** from the menu.

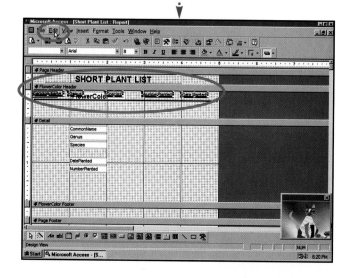

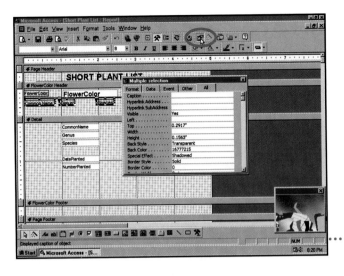

4 The newly pasted field labels are still selected. Drag them down until they are one gridline below the line drawn across the header grid. While the field labels are still selected, click the **Properties** button on the toolbar.

5 The properties sheet is displayed for the selected labels. Click the **Format** tab to view these specific properties.

Puzzled?

Remember, you can also access a property sheet for any object by double-clicking the object, or right-clicking the mouse and selecting Properties from the shortcut menu.

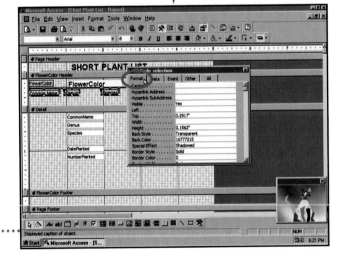

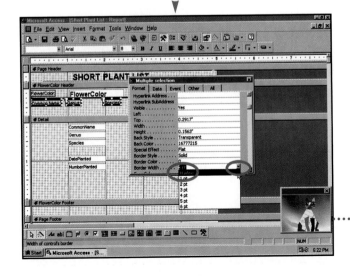

6 Select the **Special Effect** combo and click its arrow button. Choose the **Flat** option. Move to the **Border Width** combo box, and select **Hairline** from the list. Close the property sheet.

7 Select the line drawn above the labels. Press **Ctrl+C** to copy the line, and then press **Ctrl+V** to paste the copy back in the header grid. The copied line is automatically selected. Drag (the mouse pointer looks like a hand) it below the labels.

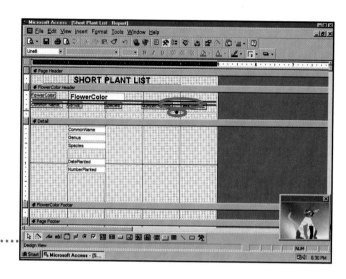

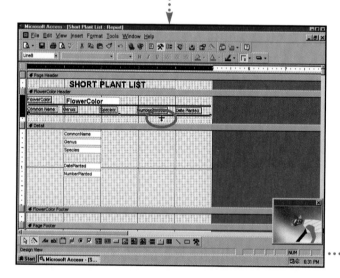

8 Now drag (the mouse pointer is a horizontal line with up and down arrows) the bottom of the FlowerColor header grid up against the new line. Access won't allow you to move it past the new line.

9 Now drag each field object underneath their respective labels. Be sure that you keep them on the Detail grid. Select the **NumberPlanted** field and drag its right side in so that the field ends at about the middle of its label.

Puzzled?

NumberPlanted is a numeric data type field, and is automatically right-aligned. If you place the right edge of this field next to the left edge of a left-aligned field, the values can be hard to read.

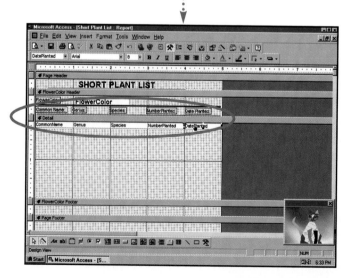

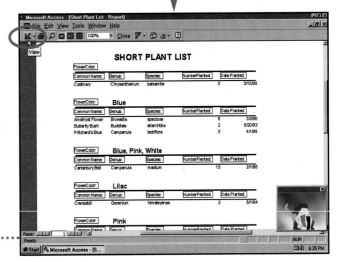

10 Place the mouse pointer at the bottom of the Detail grid and when the mouse pointer changes to a horizontal line with up and down arrows, click and drag the grid up. Keep dragging the grid up until it is snug against the field objects. Access won't allow you to drag past the fields, so don't worry about covering them up.

11 Click the **View** button to see how the report now looks. Look for potential layout problems: too much or too little space between fields and records, fields not aligned with their labels, and so on.

12 Click the Close (**X**) button and then the **Yes** button when the Office Assistant prompts you to save these changes to your form. ▪

Printing a Report

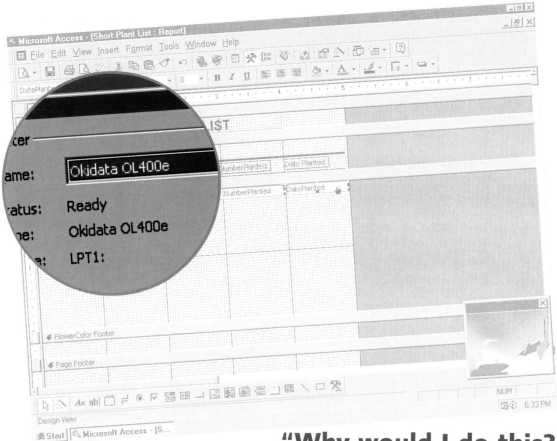

"Why would I do this?"

Once you have finished designing, refining, and checking your report format by viewing it, you are ready to show it to a larger audience. You can print a report from either the Database window, or from the Report Preview window.

1 Open the Reports list by clicking the **Reports** tab. Select the report you want to print, **Short Plant List**. Select **File, Print** from the menu.

> **Missing Link**
>
> You can also print a report by clicking the Print button on both the main toolbar and the Report Preview window's toolbar.

2 You now see the Print dialog box. You can select a printer, the number of copies to print, and how much of the report you want printed. Make your selections in the dialog box, or click the **OK** button to print one copy of the entire report.

> **Missing Link**
>
> The specific printer listed in the Name combo box will vary depending on the printers that are installed on your computer or your network.

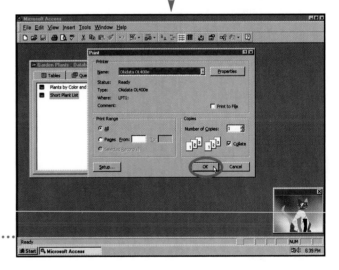

3 The Printing dialog box tells you which page is currently printing, which report is being printed, and the printer to which the print job has been sent. ■

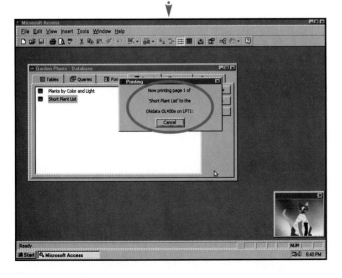

> **Puzzled?**
>
> If your printer jams, you can use the Print dialog box to print just the part of the report that didn't print. Just specify the pages you want to print by selecting the Pages option button and entering the beginning and ending page numbers in the text boxes.

231

■ ▲ ● ■ ▲ ● ■ ▲

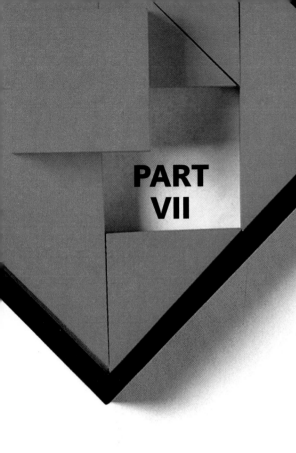

PART VII

Combining Information

63 Building a Permanent Relationship Between Tables

64 Using a Query with Two Tables

65 Creating a Report with a Query

▲ ● ■ ▲ ● ■ ▲ ●

YOU HAVE NOW LEARNED TO CREATE and use most of the objects commonly used with an Access database. In this part, you will now learn to combine information from multiple tables, a procedure that is one of the most powerful features of a *relational database* such as Access. As you built your database of tables, you included the ability to create relationships between tables by using key fields. You did this when you included a primary key field in the Plant Suppliers table with the SupplierID field, and in the Plants table with the PlantID field. By editing the Plants table so that it included a field called SupplierID, and ensuring that it used a compatible data type, you're adding a *foreign key* field to the Plants table, linking it to the Plant Suppliers table. By then linking these fields—in the Relationships window —you can create a relationship between these tables.

By combining information from several different tables, you can provide yourself, your users, and your company many powerful features that can be used every day.

The most common Access method to combine information is a query. You can use a query as a funnel to pull information from two or more sources and then display the data in a form or report. This process also works equally well in reverse. You can use a form that is based on a query to update and add records to each of the tables on which the query is based. For example, you can create a form that displays information about a supplier, enables you to add a new supplier, and a new plant—all from a single form on your screen. This is usually accomplished through the use of a *subform,* which is embedded in a master form. The subform contains a part of the job, such as the supplier information; while the master form contains the remaining information. This same technique can be applied to a customer and their purchases on an invoice.

In order for Access to use a relationship between tables or queries, you must define that relationship. You can create both permanent and temporary relationships; permanent relations are created in the Access Relationships window. Temporary relationships are created in the Query Design view and are setup between two or more tables when you use them in a query. Any relationship created in the Query Design view is only available to that query and to any objects (forms, reports, and other queries) which are based on the query. There are several types of relationships that you can create:

One-to-many relationships are the most common type of relationships. This type of relationship can exist between two tables where any one record of one table may be linked to one or more records in the other table. The relationship between a customer table and an orders table is an example of this relationship: for each customer record there can be many orders, but for each order there can be only one customer.

One-to-one relationships require that, for each record in one table, there is either one or no corresponding record in the second table. This relationship is not common. If you have tables with this type of a relationship, you may be able to combine them rather than creating a relationship. On the other hand, you may want to divide a table with a great number of fields into two or more tables that have a one-to-one relationship; or you might divide a table that contains sensitive information into a public and a private table.

Many-to-many relationships mean that for any one record of a table there can be many corresponding records in the second table, while at the same time, any one record from the second table may also have many matching records in the first table. *You should avoid this type of relationship as it can give you unpredictable results.*

The bridge table's purpose is to break the many-to-many relationship into two one-to-many relationships. A bridge table uses a *composite primary key*. A composite primary key is used when no one field is unique by itself. When building a bridge table, you usually create the composite primary key by using the primary key fields from each of the tables you want to bridge. In the sample database provided with Access, Northwind, the table "Order Details" is an excellent example of a bridge table between the Orders and Products table.

235

Building a Permanent Relationship Between Tables

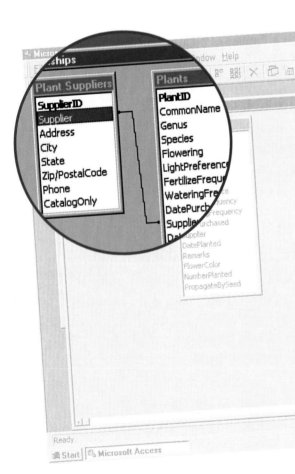

"Why would I do this?"

Permanent relationships are created between tables that each have a field whose data type is compatible with the other, and where the data from one table can be matched to information contained in the other. A permanent relationship between tables provides an automatic link when you build forms, queries, and reports. You don't have to recreate temporary relationships through a query each time you need to establish a relationship.

A permanent relationship also provides you with referential integrity. For example, a permanent relationship can be created between an orders table and a customer table where referential integrity is enforced. This means that you cannot add a new order unless it is assigned to a valid customer. This cross checking helps to ensure the validity of the data that is entered into your database.

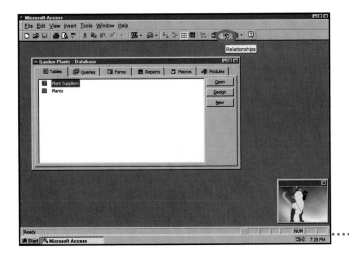

1 Open the **Garden Plants** database, if not already opened, and click on the **Relationships** button on the toolbar.

2 The Show Table dialog box appears with the Relationships window in the background. Select the **Plant Suppliers** table and click the **Add** button. You'll see the table field list appear in the Relationships window. Now select and add the **Plants** table, and then click the **Close** button to remove the Show Table dialog box.

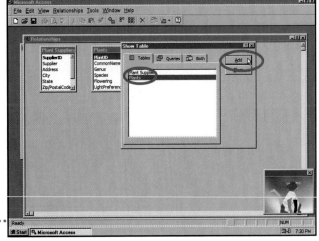

3 Increase the size of the Plants field list by dragging the bottom edge down. Move the mouse pointer to the Plant Suppliers field list and click on the **Supplier** field. Drag this field to the Plants field list and drop it onto the **Supplier** field name.

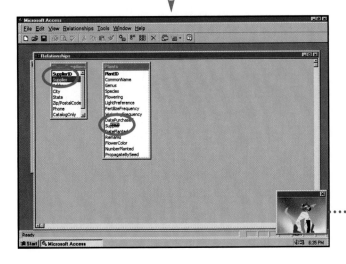

Missing Link

The Supplier field is used for these two tables because it is the only field which is common to both.

4 The Relationships dialog box appears. Click the **Create** button; Access will create a permanent relationship between these tables.

Puzzled?

The field you first selected should appear on the left side while the field name that it was dropped on should appear on the right side. If not, use the combo box arrow and select the correct field from the list.

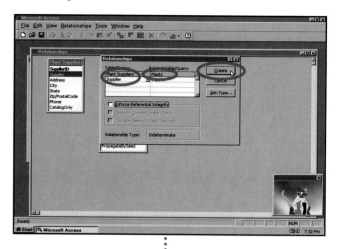

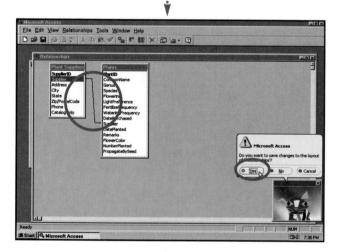

5 If Access runs into any problems when trying to create a relationship, the Office Assistant will tell you there was a problem and offer some additional assistance. Close the Relationship window, being sure to save the layout when prompted by the Office Assistant. ■

Missing Link

You can add additional tables to the relationship layout at any time, or delete relationships by selecting the relation line with the mouse and pressing the **Delete** key. To view existing properties of a relationship, double-click with the mouse on the relationship line between the two tables.

Using a Query with Two Tables

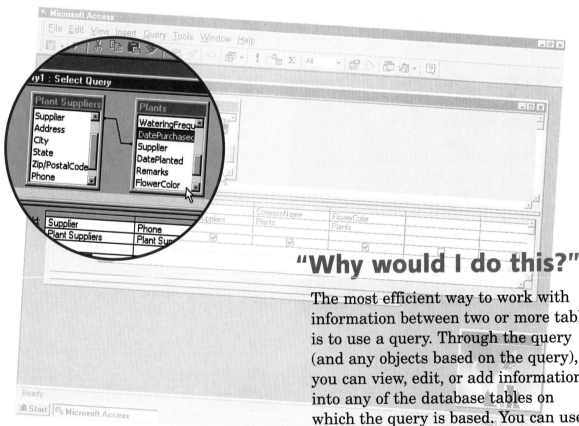

"Why would I do this?"

The most efficient way to work with information between two or more tables is to use a query. Through the query (and any objects based on the query), you can view, edit, or add information into any of the database tables on which the query is based. You can use a query to funnel information from many sources, through one point, and then into the appropriate tables.

In this task, you will create a query that will display those records which are linked together in both the Plants and Plant Suppliers tables.

Task 64: Using a Query with Two Tables

1 Click the **Queries** tab on the Database window and click the **New** button. Select **Design View** and click the **OK** button. Select both the **Plant Suppliers** and **Plants** tables from the list, click the **Add** button, and then the **Close** button.

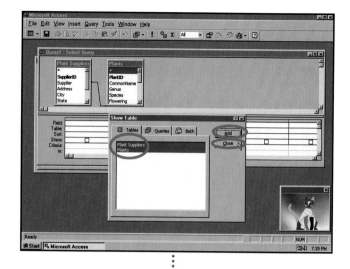

Missing Link

Notice the join-line which appears between the two table lists. This indicates that a permanent relationship has been established between these two tables.

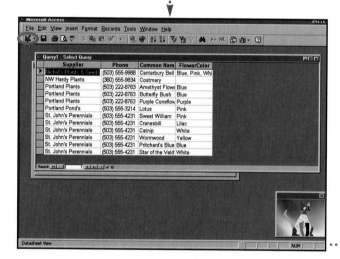

2 From the Plant Suppliers list, add the fields **Supplier** and **Phone** to the query grid, in the lower half of the screen, by double-clicking each field name. From the Plants list, add the fields **CommonName** and **FlowerColor** to the query grid. Click the **View** button to see the results set for this query.

3 You now see a single datasheet that lists all of your suppliers, their phone numbers, the plants you purchased from them, and the plants' flower colors. Click the Close (**X**) button to close the datasheet.

Puzzled?

If you see no records displayed in the results set, be sure that the supplier name in the Plant Suppliers table exactly matches the supplier name in the Suppliers field in the Plants table. Since this is the linking field, Access is looking for matching values in both tables.

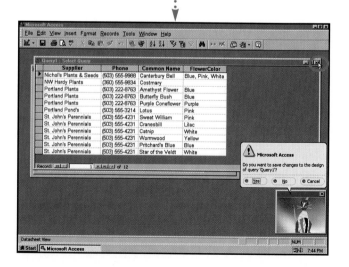

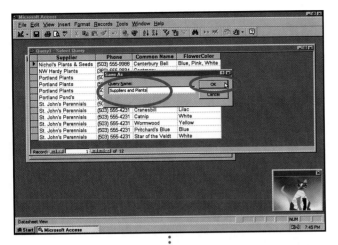

4 Select the **Yes** button when prompted by the Office Assistant to save the new query. Type **Suppliers and Plants** in the text box in the Save As dialog box, and then click the **OK** button to save your new query.

5 Your new query, Suppliers and Plants, is displayed in the Query list of the main database window. ■

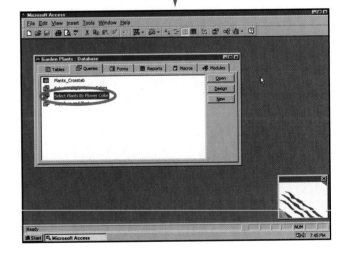

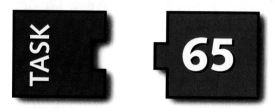

TASK 65

Creating a Report with a Query

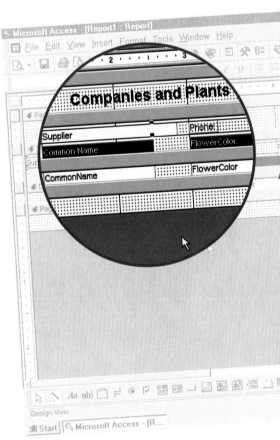

"Why would I do this?"

The best way to create many reports is by basing them on a query instead of a table. This allows you to do two things: select only those records which meet specified criteria, and combine information from multiple tables. By using a query, you can select records by customer, by time period, by product, or by several different criteria. This can help you to make your report more focused on the information that you need to present, instead of making a report so general and possibly overwhelming that crucial information and trends are lost in the details of the report.

This task will show you how to use a query to combine the information from two tables, and then to base a report on the outcome.

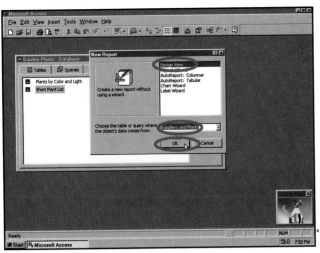

1 In the main database window, select the **Reports** tab and then click the **New** button. Select **Design View** and then the **Suppliers and Plants** query as the basis for the report. Click **OK**. Be sure to maximize the window to give yourself the most working area possible.

2 Click the **Sorting and Grouping** button displaying its dialog box. In the first row combo box, select **Supplier** by selecting it from the drop-down list. This field will be used to group the report. In the Group Properties area, select **Yes** in the Group Header combo box and then select **With First Detail** in the Keep Together combo box.

> **Missing Link**
>
> The **With First Detail** option forces Access to print a group header only if at least one detail record can also be printed on the same page.

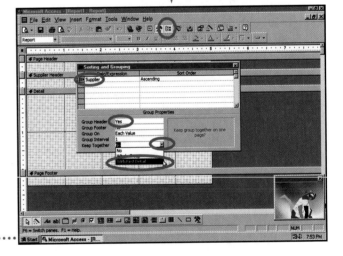

3 Move the cursor down to the next row in the top of the Sorting and Grouping dialog box and select **CommonName**. The Sort Order cell displays Ascending as the sort order. Now Access will sort the detail records in an ascending order by the CommonName field within each group. Close the dialog box.

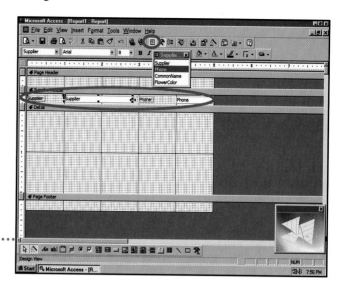

4 Open the **Field List** and place the fields **Supplier** and **Phone** in the Supplier Header grid of the report. Increase the length of the **Suppliers** field by selecting it and dragging its middle-right side handle.

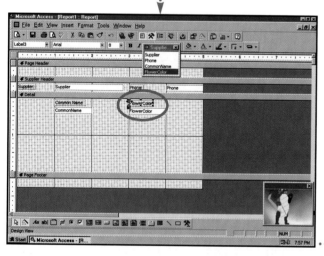

5 Select the fields **CommonName** and **FlowerColor** from the field list and drag each onto the Detail grid of the report. Close the field list and then move the attached labels above each field.

6 Select both of the attached labels; **Common Name** and **Flower Color**, and right-click the mouse to display the short-cut menu. Select the **Cut** command from the menu, removing the labels from the report and placing them on the Windows Clipboard.

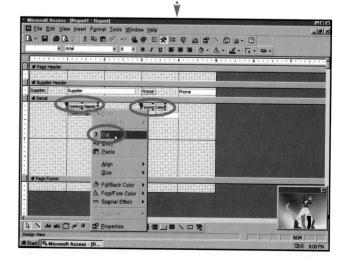

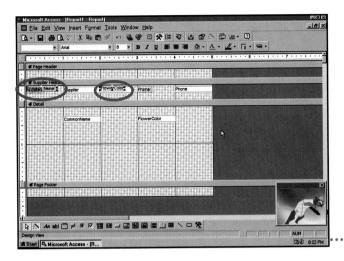

7 Move the mouse pointer to the Supplier header grid and click it once. Right-click the mouse to again display the shortcut menu, and select **Paste**. You'll see the labels appear at the top of the header grid.

8 As a group, drag the labels so that they are above their fields in the Detail grid, and then drag them down on top of the Detail bar; when you let go of the mouse, Access pushes the bar down and increases the size of the Supplier header grid.

Puzzled?

Placing the detail record labels in the group header gives you one row of labels per group; otherwise you'd have a label above each row of records, doubling the number of printed lines for the report.

9 With the FlowerColor and CommonName labels still selected, place the mouse pointer on the right edge of the **FlowerColor** label and drag it so that the field is 1½-inches long. Notice how both labels are increased in size; this is because both are still selected. Now select the **Fill/Back Color** button on the toolbar and give these two labels a black background, and then select the **Font/Fore Color** button and select white as the text color.

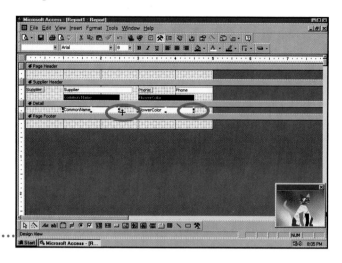

10 Select and drag both field objects on the Detail grid up against the bottom of the Detail bar and then drag the Supplier footer bar up against the bottom of the fields. Drag the right edge of one of these fields so that their size matches their labels.

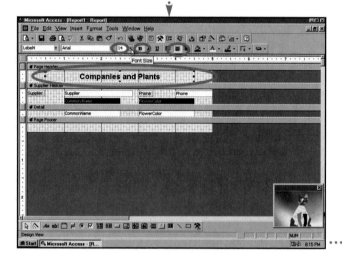

11 Select the **Label** tool from the toolbox and place a label on the Page Header grid. Type **Companies and Plants** and press the **Enter** key then click the **Bold** and **Center** icons on the toolbar, and increase the font size to **14**. This bold, centered, and enlarged header will print at the top of each page of the report.

12 Click the **Line** tool and draw two lines, one above and one below the Supplier and Phone fields on the Supplier header grid. Click the arrow part of the **Line/Border Width** button and choose the **1-pt** button. Click the **View** button.

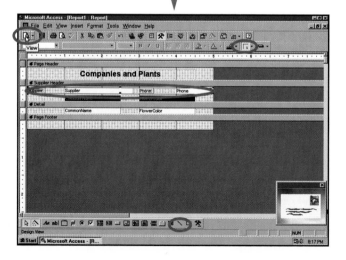

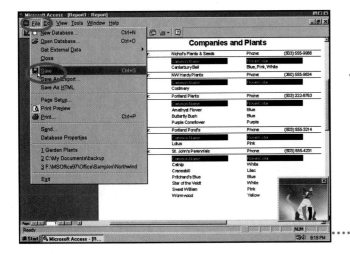

13 Be sure to check the sort order of your groups, the alignment of detail records and their labels, and the page layout. Make any corrections that may be necessary. Select **File**, **Save** from the menu.

14 In the Save As dialog box, type **Companies and Plants** in the Report Name text box, and click the **OK** button to save your new report. Since this report is based on a query, each time that you print or view the report, the query will automatically run so that your information will be as up-to-date as possible. Click the Close (**X**) button on the window. ∎

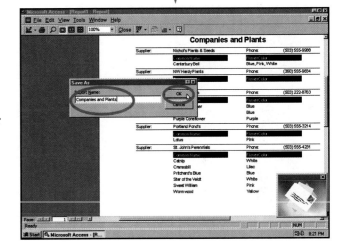

Missing Link

Remember, you can also save the report by pressing the keyboard shortcut, **Ctrl+S**, or you can return to the Design view window, and using the Save button.

Index

Symbols

* (asterisk), wild card characters, 195
* (multiply) operator, 204
+ (plus) operator, 204
- (minus) operator, 204
= (equal) operator, 204
? (question mark), wild card characters, 195

A

Access 97
  desktop shortcuts, building, 38
  exiting, 36
  Filter by Form feature, 115-117
  Filter feature, 113-114
  installing, 10-12
  launching, 14
  menu commands, utilizing, 19-21
  online help system, launching, 25-29
  Table Wizard, 49-53
  toolbars, 22

Access Relationships window, 235
action queries, 184
Add/Remove button, 12
Add/Remove Programs Properties dialog box, 11
adding
  fields to tables, 54-56, 76
  list boxes in forms, 154-155
  pop-up tip text in forms, 167-169
Apply Filter button, 114-117
applying special effects
  fields, 223
  reports, 220
arithmetic operators
  equal (=), 204
  greater than (>), 204
  less than (<), 204
  minus (-), 204
  multiply (*), 204
  plus (+), 204

AutoForms
  forms, creating, 134-135
  options
    columnar, 133
    datasheet, 133
    tabular, 133
AutoReport (Columnar), 210
AutoReport (Tabular), 210

B

Border Width button, 224
bridge tables, composite primary keys, 235
building
  desktop shortcuts, 38
  permanent relationships in tables, 236-238
  reports (Design view), 217-220
building option buttons, 163-165

buttons
- Add/Remove, 12
- Apply Filter, 114-117
- Border Width, 224
- Combo Box, 150
- Continue, 12
- Control Wizard, 150
- Create, 48
- Design, 74
- Display, 29
- Field List, 143
- Fill/Back Color, 245
- Filter by Form, 116
- Filter by Selection, 114
- Find First, 106
- Find Next, 107
- Finish, 12
- Font Size, 219
- Font/Fore Color, 245
- Help Topics, 28
- Install, 11
- Label, 147
- Line/Border Width, 246
- List, 24
- Maximize, 215
- Microsoft Access, 16
- New Object, 134-135
- New Record, 175
- Open Database, 50
- Relationships, 237
- Remove Filter, 117
- Rename, 52
- Restart Windows, 13
- Search, 35
- Sort Ascending, 112
- Sorting and Grouping, 222, 243
- Start, 11
- Table tab, 23
- Transparent button, 223
- Undo, 101

C

changing field names, 67-69
characters, database names, 46
columns
- fields, renaming, 67-69
- freezing, 123-124
- hiding, 126
- tables, resizing, 120
- unfreezing, 123-124
- unhiding, 126
Combo Box button, 150

combo boxes, forms, inserting, 149-151
commands
- Edit menu
  - Cut, 226
  - Delete Column, 77
  - Find, 103-107
  - Paste, 226
  - Replace, 108-110
  - Undo Saved Record, 100
- File menu
  - Exit, 37
  - Print, 231
  - Save, 64
- Format menu
  - Freeze Columns, 124-125
  - Hide Columns, 127
  - Unfreeze All Columns, 125
  - Unhide All Columns, 127

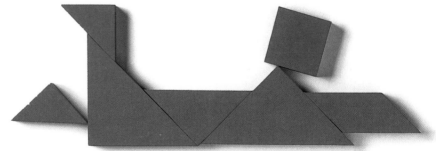

Index

Help menu
Contents and
Index, 26
What's This?, 31
View menu
Database
Objects, 21
Header/Footer,
147
composite primary keys,
235
Contents and Index com-
mand (Help menu), 26
context sensitive help, 30
Continue button, 12
Control Wizards button,
150
copying data in records,
94-96
Create button, 48
creating
databases, 46
forms
AutoForm,
134-135
Form Wizard,
133
labels
forms, 146-148
reports, 225
reports, 210
queries, 242-246
Report Wizard,
212-215
select queries,
186-190
tables from scratch,
80-82

crosstab queries, 184
implementing,
191-194
Crosstab Query dialog
box, 192
customizing
labels, 227
toolbars, 22
Cut command (Edit
menu), 226
cutting labels, 226

D

data
fields, editing, 97-99
records, copying,
94-96
searching databases,
103-107
tables
entering, 90, 92
replacing,
108-110
Database Object com-
mand (View menu), 21
databases
creating, 46
disk storage, 46
fields, defined, 8
information
dividing, 45
searching,
103-107
naming, character
maximum, 46

numeric data types,
utilizing, 57-59
opening, 18
tables, 65-66
overview, 8-9
records, defined, 8
selecting, 18
tables, defined, 8
defining relationships in
tables, 235
Delete Column command
(Edit menu), 77
deleting
fields in tables, 78-79
selected records, 118
Design button, 74
Design view
adding fields, 54-56,
76
creating reports,
217-220
designing
forms (FormsWizard),
136-139
queries, 185
tables (Table
Wizard),
49-53
desktop shortcuts,
building, 38
dialog boxes
Add/Remove
Program
Properties, 11
Crosstab Query, 192
Find, 104
Help Topics, 26

Index, 28
New Form, 137
New Query, 192
New Report, 213, 218
New Table, 50
Office Assistant, 33
Print, 231
Relationships, 238
Rename Field, 52
Replace, 109
Save As, 171
Show Table, 187, 237
Sorting and Grouping, 221-224
Topics Found, 29
Unhide All Columns, 127
Display button, 29
displaying multiple toolbars, 22
dividing information in databases, 45

E

Edit menu commands
Cut, 226
Delete Column, 77
Find, 103-107
Paste, 226
Replace, 108-110
Undo Saved Record, 100

editing
data
fields, 97-99
forms, 174-177
forms, 140-141
labels in forms, 161-162
edits, undoing, 100-102
entering
data
forms, 174-177
tables, 90-92
text, labels, 146-148
executing Yes/No responses in fields, 60-62
existing databases, opening, 18
Exit command (File menu), 37
exiting
Access, 36
Office Assistant, 35

F

Field List button, 143
fields
applying special effects, 223
data changes, undoing, 100-102
defined, 8
editing data, 97-99

forms
inserting, 142-145
moving, 158
ordering, 178-179
linking tables, 45
names, changing, 67-69
naming, 54-56
records, 44
renaming, 52
reports, sorting, 221-224
sorting reports, 221-224
tables
adding, 54-56, 76
deleting, 78-79
inserting, 73
moving, 70
Yes/No responses, executing, 60-62
File menu commands
Exit, 37
Print, 231
Save, 64
Fill/Back Color button, 245
Filter by Form button, 116
Filter by Form feature, 115-117
Filter by Selection button, 114

filters, records, implementing, 113-117

Find button, 104

Find command (Edit menu), 103-107

Find dialog box, 104

Find First button, 106

Find Next button, 107

Finish button, 12

Font Size button, 219

Font/Fore Color button, 245

foreign keys in tables, 44

Form Design view
  forms, editing, 140-141
  launching, 140-141

Form Wizard forms
  creating, 133
  designing, 136-139

Format menu commands
  Freeze Columns, 124
  Hide Columns, 127
  Unfreeze All Columns, 125
  Unhide All Columns, 127

forms
  adding
    list boxes, 154-155
    pop-up tip text, 167-169

building option buttons, 163-165

creating
  AutoForm, 134-135
  Form Wizard, 133
  labels, 146-148

data
  editing, 174-177
  entering, 174-177

defined, 132

designing with Form Wizard, 136-139

editing, 140-141
  data, 174-177
  labels, 161-162

entering data, 174-177

inserting
  combo boxes, 149-151
  fields, 142-145

moving fields, 158

opening, 172-173

ordering fields, 178-179

saving, 170-171

uses, 132

Freeze Columns command (Format menu), 124

freezing columns, 123-124

G - H - I

grouping fields in reports, 221-224

Header/Footer command (View menu), 147

Help menu commands
  Content and Index, 26
  What's This?, 31

Help system (online)
  context-sensitive, 30
  find command, 25-29
  indexes, 25-29
  launching Access 97, 25-29
  Office Assistant, 32
  table of contents, 25-29

Help Topics button, 28

Help Topics dialog box, 26

Hide Columns command (Format menu), 127

hiding columns, 126

implementing
  crosstab queries, 191-194
  filters in records, 113-117

Index dialog box, 28

indexes, online help system, 25-29

information, dividing in databases, 45

inserting
combo boxes in forms, 149-151
fields
forms, 142-145
tables, 73
Install button, 11
installing Access 97, 10-12

L

Label button, 147
Label Wizard features, 210
labels
customizing, 227
cutting, 226
forms
creating, 146-148
editing, 161-162
pasting, 226
reports, creating, 225
text, entering, 146-148
launching
Access, 14
online help system, 25-29
Form Design view window, 140-141

Microsoft Office Professional CD, 11
Office Assistant, 32
Report Wizard, 213
Line Border Width button, 246
linking tables with primary eys, 45
list boxes, forms, adding, 154-155
List button, 24

M

Maximize button, 215
Menu commands, utilizing, 19-21
Microsoft Office Professional CD, launching, 11
modifying
field order in forms, 178-179
numeric data types, 57-59
moving fields
forms, 158
tables, 70
multiple criteria, selecting for records, 201
multiple tables, creating queries, 239-240

N

naming
databases, 46
fields, 54-56
changing, 67-69
New Form dialog box, 137
New Object button, 134-135
New Query dialog box, 192
New Record button, 175
New Report dialog box, 213-218
New Table dialog box, 50
numeric data types
modifying, 58-59
utilizing, 57-59

O

objects, creating in forms, 134-135
Office Assistant
exiting, 35
features, 32
launching, 32
Office Assistant dialog box, 33
Open database button, 50
opening
databases, 18
forms, 172-173
tables, 65-66

operating
   numeric data types
      in databases, 57-59
   tab buttons, 23-24
operators, OR, 198-200
option buttons, forms,
   building, 163-165
OR operator, selecting
   records, 198-200
ordering fields in
   forms, 178-179

P

Paste command (Edit
   menu), 226
pasting labels, 226
permanent relationships
   referential integrity,
      236-238
   tables, building,
      236-238
pop-up tip text, forms,
   adding, 167-169
previewing reports, 215
primary keys, linking
   tables, 45
Print command (File
   menu), 231
Print dialog box, 231
printing reports, 230
Program Install
   Wizard, 11

Q - R

queries
   action, 184
   creating
      multiple tables,
         239-240
      reports, 242-246
   crosstab, 184
      implementing,
         191-194
   designing, 185
   multiple tables, 239
   relationships,
      defining, 235
   select, 184
      creating,
         186-190

records
   copying data, 94-96
   data changes,
      undoing, 100-102
   defined, 8
   fields, 44
   implementing
      filters, 113-117
   multiple criteria,
      selecting, 201
   OR operator, select-
      ing, 198-200
   relational database
      management
      system, 44
   selected,
      deleting, 118
   tables, sorting, 111
   wild-card characters,
      selecting, 195-196

referential integrity,
   236-238
Relational database man-
   agement system, 44
Relational databases,
   defining tables, 235
Relationships button, 237
Relationships
   dialog box, 238
Remove Filter
   button, 117
Rename button, 52
Rename Field
   dialog box, 52
renaming
   column labels in
      fields, 67-69
   fields, 52
Replace command (Edit
   menu), 108-110
Replace dialog box, 109
replacing data in tables,
   108-110
Report Wizard
   creating reports,
      212-215
   features, 210
   launching, 213
reports
   Chart Wizard
      features, 210
   creating, 210
      labels, 225
      Design view
         building,
            217-220

reports *(cont)*
  Label Wizard
    features, 210
  overview, 210
  previewing, 215
  printing, 230
  queries, creating,
    242-246
  Report Wizard,
    creating, 212-215
  special effects,
    applying, 220
  uses, 210
resizing
  columns in
    tables, 120
  rows in tables, 120
Restart Windows
  button, 13
result sets in queries, 185
rows, tables, resizing, 120

S

Save As dialog box, 171
Save command (File
  menu), 64
saving
  forms, 170-171
  tables, definition, 63
Search button, 35
searching information in
  databases, 103-107
select queries, 184
  creating, 186-190
selected records,
  deleting, 118

selecting
  databases, 18
  records
    multiple crite-
      ria, 201
    OR operator,
      198-200
    wild-card char-
      acters, 195-196
Show Table dialog
  box, 187, 237
Sort Ascending
  button, 112
sorting
  fields in reports,
    221-224
  records in tables, 111
Sorting and Grouping
  button, 222, 243
Sorting and Grouping
  dialog box, 221-224
special effects
  applying to
    reports, 220
  fields, applying, 223
Start button, 11
Start Microsoft Access
  button, 16
storing databases, 46

T

Tab buttons,
  operating, 23-24
Table of contents, online
  help system, 25-29

Table Wizard
  features, 49-53
  tables, designing,
    49-53
tables
  adding fields,
    54-56, 76
  building permanent
    relationships,
    236-238
  creating from
    scratch, 80-82
  defined, 8
  definition, saving, 63
  deleting fields, 78-79
  designing with
    TableWizard, 49-53
  entering data, 90, 92
  fields, renaming,
    67-69
  foreign keys, 44
  inserting fields, 73
  linking fields, 45
  moving
    fields, 70
    opening, 65-66
  primary keys, 44
    linking, 45
  record
    filtering, 113-114
  referential
    integrity, 236-238

tables *(cont)*

    relational database management system, 44

    relationships, defining, 235

    replacing data, 108-110

    resizing

        columns, 120

        rows, 120

    sorting records, 111

    utilizing in queries, 239

    Yes/No responses, utilizing, 60-62

Tables tab button, 23

text

    entering in labels, 146-148

    pop-up help, adding, 167-169

toolbars

    Access 22

    customizing, 22

    multiple, displaying, 22

Toolbars command (View menu), 20

Topics Found dialog box, 29

Transparent button, 223

U - V

Undo button, 101

Undo Saved Record command (Edit menu), 100

undoing data changes in records, 100-102

Unfreeze All Columns command (Format menu), 125

unfreezing columns, 123-124

Unhide All Columns command (Format menu), 127

Unhide All Columns dialog box, 127

unhiding columns, 126

View menu commands

    Database Object, 21

    Header/Footer, 147

    Toolbars, 20

W- X - Y - Z

What's This? command (Help menu), 31

Wild-card characters

    asterisk (*), 195

    question mark (?), 195

    selecting in records, 195-196

Yes/No responses, executing, 60-62

Check out Que® Books on the World Wide Web
http://www.mcp.com/que

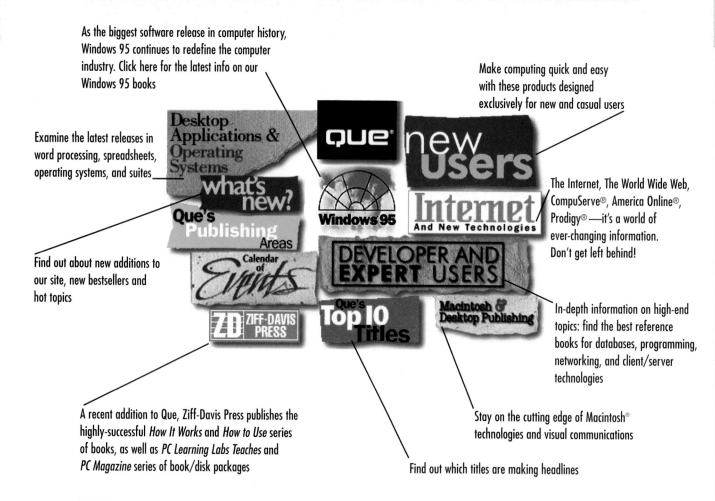

As the biggest software release in computer history, Windows 95 continues to redefine the computer industry. Click here for the latest info on our Windows 95 books

Make computing quick and easy with these products designed exclusively for new and casual users

Examine the latest releases in word processing, spreadsheets, operating systems, and suites

The Internet, The World Wide Web, CompuServe®, America Online®, Prodigy® —it's a world of ever-changing information. Don't get left behind!

Find out about new additions to our site, new bestsellers and hot topics

In-depth information on high-end topics: find the best reference books for databases, programming, networking, and client/server technologies

A recent addition to Que, Ziff-Davis Press publishes the highly-successful *How It Works* and *How to Use* series of books, as well as *PC Learning Labs Teaches* and *PC Magazine* series of book/disk packages

Stay on the cutting edge of Macintosh® technologies and visual communications

Find out which titles are making headlines

With 6 separate publishing groups, Que develops products for many specific market segments and areas of computer technology. Explore our Web Site and you'll find information on best-selling titles, newly published titles, upcoming products, authors, and much more.

- Stay informed on the latest industry trends and products available
- Visit our online bookstore for the latest information and editions
- Download software from Que's library of the best shareware and freeware

MICROSOFT® OFFICE 97 RESOURCE CENTER

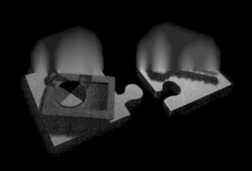

For the most up-to-date information about all the Microsoft Office 97 products, visit Que's Web Resource Center at

http://www.mcp.com/que/msoffice

The web site extends the reach of this Que book by offering you a rich selection of supplementary content.

You'll find information about Que books as well as additional content about these new **Office 97 topics**:

- **Word**
- **Excel**
- **PowerPoint®**
- **Visual Basic® for Applications**
- **Access**
- **Outlook™**
- **FrontPage™**

Visit Que's web site regularly for a variety of new and updated Office 97 information.

The best resources and tips for getting things done with Office 97!

Complete and Return this Card
for a *FREE* Computer Book Catalog

Thank you for purchasing this book! You have purchased a superior computer book written expressly for your needs. To continue to provide the kind of up-to-date, pertinent coverage you've come to expect from us, we need to hear from you. Please take a minute to complete and return this self-addressed, postage-paid form. In return, we'll send you a free catalog of all our computer books on topics ranging from word processing to programming and the internet.

Mr. ☐   Mrs. ☐   Ms. ☐   Dr. ☐

Name (first) ☐☐☐☐☐☐☐☐☐☐☐☐   (M.I.) ☐   (last) ☐☐☐☐☐☐☐☐☐☐☐☐☐☐☐☐

Address ☐☐☐☐☐☐☐☐☐☐☐☐☐☐☐☐☐☐☐☐☐☐☐☐☐☐☐☐☐☐☐☐☐☐☐☐

☐☐☐☐☐☐☐☐☐☐☐☐☐☐☐☐☐☐☐☐☐☐☐☐☐☐☐☐☐☐☐☐☐☐☐☐

City ☐☐☐☐☐☐☐☐☐☐☐☐☐   State ☐☐   Zip ☐☐☐☐☐ ☐☐☐☐

Phone ☐☐☐ ☐☐☐ ☐☐☐☐   Fax ☐☐☐ ☐☐☐ ☐☐☐☐

Company Name ☐☐☐☐☐☐☐☐☐☐☐☐☐☐☐☐☐☐☐☐☐☐☐☐☐☐☐☐☐☐☐

E-mail address ☐☐☐☐☐☐☐☐☐☐☐☐☐☐☐☐☐☐☐☐☐☐☐☐☐☐☐☐☐☐

1. Please check at least (3) influencing factors for purchasing this book.

Front or back cover information on book .... ☐
Special approach to the content .... ☐
Completeness of content .... ☐
Author's reputation .... ☐
Publisher's reputation .... ☐
Book cover design or layout .... ☐
Index or table of contents of book .... ☐
Price of book .... ☐
Special effects, graphics, illustrations .... ☐
Other (Please specify): _____ ☐

2. How did you first learn about this book?

Saw in Macmillan Computer Publishing catalog .... ☐
Recommended by store personnel .... ☐
Saw the book on bookshelf at store .... ☐
Recommended by a friend .... ☐
Received advertisement in the mail .... ☐
Saw an advertisement in: _____ ☐
Read book review in: _____ ☐
Other (Please specify): _____ ☐

3. How many computer books have you purchased in the last six months?

This book only .... ☐   3 to 5 books .... ☐
2 books .... ☐   More than 5 .... ☐

4. Where did you purchase this book?

Bookstore .... ☐
Computer Store .... ☐
Consumer Electronics Store .... ☐
Department Store .... ☐
Office Club .... ☐
Warehouse Club .... ☐
Mail Order .... ☐
Direct from Publisher .... ☐
Internet site .... ☐
Other (Please specify): _____ ☐

5. How long have you been using a computer?

☐ Less than 6 months   ☐ 6 months to a year
☐ 1 to 3 years   ☐ More than 3 years

6. What is your level of experience with personal computers and with the subject of this book?

	With PCs	With subject of book
New	☐	☐
Casual	☐	☐
Accomplished	☐	☐
Expert	☐	☐

Source Code ISBN: 0-7897-1027-7

7. Which of the following best describes your job title?

Administrative Assistant .... ☐
Coordinator .... ☐
Manager/Supervisor .... ☐
Director .... ☐
Vice President .... ☐
President/CEO/COO .... ☐
Lawyer/Doctor/Medical Professional .... ☐
Teacher/Educator/Trainer .... ☐
Engineer/Technician .... ☐
Consultant .... ☐
Not employed/Student/Retired .... ☐
Other (Please specify): _____ ☐

8. Which of the following best describes the area of the company your job title falls under?

Accounting .... ☐
Engineering .... ☐
Manufacturing .... ☐
Operations .... ☐
Marketing .... ☐
Sales .... ☐
Other (Please specify): _____ ☐

9. What is your age?

Under 20 .... ☐
21-29 .... ☐
30-39 .... ☐
40-49 .... ☐
50-59 .... ☐
60-over .... ☐

10. Are you:

Male .... ☐
Female .... ☐

11. Which computer publications do you read regularly? (Please list)

_____
_____
_____
_____
_____
_____
_____
_____
_____
_____

Comments: _____
_____
_____

Fold here and scotch-tape to mail.